In the financial services industry, service is a key element for success. In *Lessons From the Mouse*, you will get practical solutions to deliver exceptional service and the lessons can be applied at all levels within the organization.

**—Thomas E. Hoaglin**
*CEO - Huntington Bank*

Dennis Snow has hit another home run. *Lessons From the Mouse* is unique. It is an easy read, but packed with practical business wisdom. Dennis' "lessons" apply to anyone, anywhere, at any time. Read it and reap the benefits for your organization and yourself.

**— Allan R. Nagle**
*Former President, Tupperware Worldwide,*
*Former Interim Dean,*
*Crummer School of Business, Rollins College*

The principles outlined in *Lessons From the Mouse*, while based upon Dennis' experience at Walt Disney World, translate to any organization and any individual within an organization. Cummins is successfully applying these principles globally to create great experiences for customers and to enable every employee to have a clear line of sight to the customer.

**— Joe Loughrey**
*President and Chief Operating Officer,*
*Cummins Inc.*

Dennis Snow teaches how to show empathy, pay attention to detail, have fun, go the extra mile, and listen to your customers — all things that cost nothing to deliver but say, "we care," which is the most important message you can send.

**—Dave Baca**
*Managing Partner,*
*Law Offices of Davis Wright Tremaine LLP*

*Lessons From the Mouse* offers what our front line team members value most — practical, actionable, relatable solutions to the everyday issues and opportunities they face with customers. Dennis knows what matters to the customer and he presents solid ideas for making their experience memorable. No fancy theories, just simple wisdom that works. It's a worthwhile read!

— **Roberto R. Herencia**
*President,*
*Banco Popular North America*

What makes *Lessons From the Mouse* so valuable is that Dennis Snow writes from a front line, customer contact perspective. There's no wasted space in this book. Every page has ideas ready to put to work for you or your organization. *Lessons From the Mouse* is engaging, entertaining, and of great practical value. This is a winner!

—**Joe Calloway**
*Author,*
***Work Like You're Showing Off!***

At Florida State University we have found the principles of *Lessons From the Mouse* to be very useful in the service we provide to students and their families. Dennis Snow's leadership tips encourage you to take ownership of your institution's mission, regardless of your role. "***Lessons***" also provides excellent advice for our new college graduates as they begin their first jobs.

—**Mary B. Coburn**
*Vice President for Student Affairs*
*Florida State University*

I read the book in one sitting on a rainy afternoon in Central Illinois. I expected to read "another customer service book" and trust me I feel as though I have read them all. Much to my surprise, this book is truly different. The title tells you exactly what you are going to achieve from reading this book: lessons. Not cute mnemonics, not another pillar of success story or even one filled with cute jargon written to humor and not teach. **Lessons From the Mouse** approaches customer service with tried and true information from one of the world's best at delivery and execution of service excellence, Walt Disney! The stories are written from the perspective of an employee: how it felt to be hired by Disney, what orientation was really like, the difference between "onstage" and "off stage" and what lessons employees who leave Disney take with them for life. This book shows you that Disney examples have universal application to all businesses. Finally, I feel as though I have found a book with universal application to customer service. This book will not be sitting within my library with the others; I plan to use it as a text book for our service initiative. Thank you for the ten easy to follow lessons and for sharing your lessons with us.

—**Carolyn Otten**
*Chief Operating Officer*
*Springfield Clinic LLP*

Dennis Snow has built a better mousetrap, capturing the best ideas from his years with Walt Disney World and sharing them with anyone interested in improving his or her organization or career. By mastering his simple **Lessons From the Mouse**, any company—and any employee—can become well known for extraordinary customer service.

—**Ed Yingling**
*President and CEO*
*American Bankers Association*

The culture of a company matters and Disney is likely the pre-eminent example of this mantra. However this book is not a manual with a magic formula to create Disney-like companies worldwide. Rather Dennis Snow develops concepts couched in real life examples about how to keep the focus on the customer. Focus on the customer, of course, always has the added and considerable benefit of creating fully engaged associates at all levels and value for shareholders. The lessons here are concrete and accessible but not easy. If incorporated into a business and into personal life they will lead to significant change. Change that is worth the effort.

—**Melvin F. Hall, Ph.D.**
*President & CEO*
*Press Ganey Associates, Inc.*

# LESSONS
## from the
# MOUSE

**A Guide for Applying Disney World's
Secrets of Success to Your Organization,
Your Career, and Your Life**

By

## Dennis Snow

 Snow & Associates, Inc.

ORLANDO • FLORIDA

Snow & Associates, Inc.
3461 Bellington Drive
Orlando, FL 32835
TEL: 407.294.1855
Fax: 407.522.1939
info@snowassociates.com

Book set in Janson Text
Cover Design and Composition by Jonathan Pennell

Library of Congress Catalog Number: 2010906973
        Snow. Dennis,
Lessons From the Mouse: A Guide for Applying Disney World's Secrets of Success to Your Organization, Your Career, and Your Life

        ISBN: 978-0-615-37241-9
First Snow & Associates, Inc. Edition
25    24    23    22    21    20    19    18    17
Printed in the United States of America

*To Marie and Dick Snow; the most wonderful parents and role models a son could hope for. Thanks for taking me on my first visit to Disney World. Who knew?*

# Contents

# Introduction

I had just become an employee at Walt Disney World — or, as they say at Disney, a cast member. Imagine how exciting this was for me, an eager nineteen-year-old steeped in Disney lore and now wide eyed at the start of new-hire training. It was the summer of 1979. I had just finished a year of college and thought it would be pretty cool to work at Disney World. I was ready for some magic. So, I hopped in my beat-up, rusted-out Oldsmobile and headed south from Burlington, Vermont, on the twelve-hundred-mile drive to Orlando, Florida. I slept in rest areas along the way and dreamed about my grand summer adventure. At that time, I was planning to go back home in September. But I never did. I fell in love with Disney World, decided to finish my education in Florida and make Orlando home.

It wasn't love at first sight, mind you. My very first day of training was, to say the least, sadly eye opening. I was "cast" to work at the 20,000 Leagues Under the Sea attraction. We new employees were touring the park behind the scenes, and just inside the fluorescent maze beneath the Magic Kingdom, I spied Mickey Mouse entering the employee cafeteria. But it wasn't the cute, approachable Mickey I was used to seeing. This one was a dreadful hybrid, half cartoon rodent and half woman. It really was rather unsettling. Nearby, like a scene from a horror movie, the severed heads of Tigger, Goofy, and Donald Duck — frozen in artificial mirth — stood watch on special poles. Farther on in the starkly lit maze, two Jungle Cruise skippers cursed an absent co-worker. Around a corner, Cinderella, cigarette dangling from her lips, adjusted her bodice and chatted up another half-dressed Mickey. I thought, "There's more than one?"

Then, my trainer led me from behind the scenes onto the set, from Disney underground — the employee areas where guests weren't allowed — to Disney above ground — the park where guests experienced the characters, the rides and the shows. Ah! This was what I remembered! Here was the magic I had traveled so far for. Here, everything was right. Fairytale characters were totally costumed and playing their parts convincingly, floating and posing among smiling guests who clicked their cameras and lined up for Peter Pan's Flight.

That day, I began to understand Disney's magic, an understanding that deepened over the next two decades. It was, I realized, really just a blend of ordinary elements — imagination, hard work, attention to detail, and creativity. But like some preposterous confection, these commonplace ingredients were what created extraordinary experiences for Disney guests. That caught my attention.

I stayed at Disney World for twenty years. I stayed because I knew I was part of a great organization, and I knew I would learn important lessons. Now, as a customer service speaker and consultant, I find that I still use what I learned there every day.

## WHY ANOTHER DISNEY BOOK?

Several books have already been written about the Disney way, so why write another one? Good question, especially since some of those books are excellent. But I felt there was a gap in the Disney literature. Most of the books out there were written by people who had never actually worked at Disney or were written from the perspective of senior management. I thought there was a need for a Disney manual written by someone who had actually worked on the rides, controlled the crowds at parades, stood in the rain for hours telling guests Space Mountain was closed, and even had to reprimand Goofy for poor attendance. In my version, I peel away the veneer to show the day-to-day operation, warts and all. The book includes lessons I learned as a front-line cast member as well as a member of the management team.

How do I know these lessons can translate to success in other organizations? In my speaking, training, and consulting work, business leaders often tell me about one of their employees who previously worked as a Disney cast member. These leaders always rave about this employee's customer service abilities, work ethic, and attention to detail. One executive told me, "I'd love to send every one of my employees to work at Disney World for a few months."

But for me, the most meaningful example of all is that of my oldest son, Danny. I insisted he work at Disney World for a summer because I knew he'd learn things that would benefit him for the rest of his life. And I knew that having the Disney name on his resume would not be a bad thing, either. He worked at Big Thunder Mountain Railroad in Frontierland that summer, and it was great listening to him share some of the same stories I had lived during my early Disney days. When Danny went off to college at Florida State University, he worked at a retail shop in Tallahassee. I met his boss who told me: "Danny is our customer service champ. All of the customers love him." Even though he worked at Disney World for only three months, the lessons he learned there have stuck.

Over the years I've helped many organizations apply the principles in this book — the principles I was privileged to learn at Disney. The results for these companies have been positive: improved customer satisfaction; reduced employee turnover; and increased profitability. (I readily admit it hasn't worked for everyone — it takes a lot of commitment to consistently apply these lessons, and some companies just want a magic pill that will suddenly improve their culture. Sorry, it doesn't work that way.)

# IT'S NOT PERFECT

During a frustrating time early in my Disney career, my boss told me something I will never forget: "There's no such thing as a perfect boss or a perfect company. If you're looking for either one you're doomed to a life of disappointment." He was so right. At no time do I want to present the Disney organization as perfect or infallible. The company screws up just like every other organization, and, in the book, I have happily shared some of those mistakes. As I'm sure you know, Disney's blunders are pretty well publicized. The challenging departure of former CEO Michael Eisner in 2005 is a good example. Or the challenges Euro Disney faced early on. The hits the company took on those little gems were mostly well deserved.

The things Disney does well, however, it does very well. Consistent focus on a few important factors has made it stand out as a company and created legions of diehard fans. The proof is that Disney World is usually ranked the single most popular vacation destination on earth.

I'm always amazed that no matter where I travel in the world, people know Disney. At the beginning of every presentation or workshop I conduct, I always ask the attendees to raise their hands if they've been to Disney World. Invariably, the majority of the attendees raise their hands. When I ask how many have been there more than once, twice, three times, etc., plenty of hands stay up. I'm still a Disney stockholder, so I appreciate that level of loyalty.

## HOW THE BOOK IS STRUCTURED

*Lessons From the Mouse* is constructed as a series of lessons because therein lies the secret to discovering Disney's magic — understanding and applying these ideas every day in a disciplined way. I believe the elements described in this book are at the very heart of what has made the place so successful.

The title of each chapter is a snapshot of the lesson within. At the beginning of each chapter, I explain how this particular lesson was taught and reinforced when I worked at Disney World and why it's important. I then show how the lesson applies to other industries by using examples from my consulting work and from conversations with leaders and employees of other organizations. The end of each chapter provides some questions and ideas for utilizing the lesson.

## HOW TO USE THE BOOK

There are a lot of ways you can apply the lessons in this book. You might decide to use them to raise the bar of your own performance. You might decide to make each chapter a topic for a series of staff meetings to get the whole team involved. If you're really ambitious, you can use each chapter as a training module for the entire organization. Or you might simply open the book periodically to any chapter for a quick dose of inspiration. However you decide to use *Lessons From the Mouse*, the important thing is to put the lessons to work.

Anybody and any organization can employ these ideas. I've seen them applied by major research hospitals and by gas stations. I've seen bank presidents as well as truck mechanics put these principles to good use. It all comes down to commitment, consistency, and hard work.

All the best to you as you read and apply *Lessons From the Mouse*.

# Never Let Backstage Come Onstage

## BEHIND THE MAGIC

During my initial instruction at Disney World's 20,000 Leagues Under the Sea attraction, my trainer, Jeff, went to great lengths to stress the importance of preserving the Disney magic for guests. He talked about "backstage," the behind-the-scenes locations where cast members ate, drank, smoked (in those days), complained about management, gossiped about the previous night's keg party, and did what any normal person on a break would do. Backstage, Jeff indicated, was also designated for truck deliveries, costume changes, composting, company meetings, and so on — things the public was never supposed to see. Backstage, you see, was that mysterious place underneath, behind, and beyond where thousands of operations vital to running the park and to creating the illusion of magic happened. All, as I said, out of sight of the guests.

"Onstage," Jeff went on to contrast, was where the show took place. It was everything that happened on each and every stage at Disney World, and it was also everything that occurred on Main Street USA, at and around Cinderella's Castle, and every other spot you'd find a guest. Onstage was where we Disney employees had an opportunity to impress the guests. It was where spells were cast, expectations were exceeded, and magic was made. I remember as we walked from the backstage area to onstage (Disney speak for walking from a storeroom to a storefront), Jeff made a big production about whether my costume looked right and my nametag was straight. He made sure I was smiling, too. Perhaps they were a bit over the top, but his last minute onstage checks have stayed with me. Jeff knew if a guest were ever to view the backstage environment, the magic would be lost. After all, a partially dressed Mickey Mouse or stack of fifty or so trash bags could easily ruin the fantasy. The company took this notion so seriously, in fact, that Jeff warned me not ever to take anyone, even a friend or a family member, backstage for a quick peek. If I did, I would likely be fired, he said. That was a vivid message.

Later, one of my responsibilities as the first shift supervisor in Fantasyland was to make sure the area was "show ready" when the park opened. By that time, custodial cast members, painters, landscapers, and the maintenance team had been on the job for hours getting the place shipshape. My job was to double-check that everything was perfectly in order. I would arrive an hour and a half prior to opening, scan the logbook for any important notes from the previous evening's shift supervisor, and begin my regular walk-through of Fantasyland.

Sometimes I found little problems like burned-out light bulbs, a dirty bench, or a speaker that wasn't working properly. Occasionally, the landscaping team had left a shovel behind, or a maintenance worker had forgotten a ladder. The evening crew always had quite a lot of work to do, and sometimes little items like these were missed. Many of the smaller items, like a left behind shovel or ladder, I would simply take care of myself. Larger pieces of equipment such as a generator might require a call to the Maintenance Department. One way or another, these items were taken care of before the first guests entered the park.

A couple of discoveries, though, I kept to myself. One time, I found a dead chipmunk lying in front of Peter Pan's Flight. Lest it cause undue concern for the lives of our own beloved pair of chipmunks, Chip and Dale, I hastily disposed of the real one. Another time, I found a pair of men's boxer shorts beneath the flying boats at the same ride. (Hmm. People definitely interpret Disney magic in a lot of different ways.)

Sometimes an outside vendor was hired to do maintenance work, and as opening time approached it fell to me to tell the contracted crew it was time to move their equipment backstage. Well, outside workers simply didn't get the idea of onstage and backstage, and inevitably arguments arose. Warnings like, "Dust goes backstage: Pixie Dust goes onstage," didn't go over well with the average welder or roofer, as you can imagine. Eventually, though,

I was able to persuade them to move their tools and repair work backstage.

Exceptions did occur, of course. Not every maintenance job could be done after hours or behind the scenes. For example, every few years, Cinderella's Castle had to be repainted. This was a massive job that took several weeks. Certainly it would be cost and time prohibitive to bring the huge cranes and scaffolding on and off the stage every morning and evening. To maintain the magic, signs were posted informing guests about the castle restoration and apologizing for the visual intrusion. But, apology or no apology, I would cringe every time I walked past the castle when it was being painted. To see anything compromise the show we had worked so hard to pull off every day was difficult. That's how ingrained the onstage/backstage philosophy was for me, and still is. At Disney, this concept was a way of doing business that instilled employee pride in the customer's experience and in the final product.

BEING
PROUD OF
DOING THE
JOB RIGHT

When I was at Disney, this onstage/backstage philosophy was not just about physical elements: it was also about behavior. The Disney cast members I knew experienced the same frustrations and challenges as employees in other companies. They had disagreements, dissatisfaction with their pay, problems with bosses, commuting issues, and arguments with their spouses. Allowing these normal occurrences to impact the customer experience, however, was totally unacceptable. Once you were onstage, the show was on. Backstage behaviors and problems were to stay backstage. The expectation was for you to leave problems at the door at the beginning of your shift and pick them up again at the end. Like the advice of the turn-of-the-century Western bartender, "Take it outside!" But in Disney's case, it was more like, "Take it backstage!" I know this may seem rigid and unfeeling, but that's exactly what was expected and exactly what we did.

Of course, no stage, no employee, and no company is ever perfect, so backstage behaviors sometimes crept onstage. Most of the time, it was no big deal — the accidental unzipped costume, a slight disagreement between cast members, or an uncomfortably hot balloon vendor frowning in the bright sun. But, occasionally, there were more glaring examples. When I was a supervisor in the Magic Kingdom Character Department, one of my jobs was to help orchestrate the daily character parade. Weather could be a factor since the parade was held outdoors. During a light rain, it usually ran. A heavy rain, though, could severely damage the floats and costumes, so we would have to cancel the parade at those times. You can imagine guests' disappointment when this happened.

During one rainstorm, I announced to the waiting character entertainers we were canceling the parade. To my horror, they cheered — loudly enough for guests to hear. Keep in mind the parade was the most arduous part of a character entertainer's job; it was a mile of non-stop moving and dancing in heavy, hot costumes and, more often than not, in shoes twice the size of the entertainers' feet! I've done it, and I've never sweated so much in my life. So, a day of no parade was understandably appealing. I knew what the whooping applause meant, but I also knew that guests could hear the cheering. Sure enough, the complaints rolled in. They went something like this: how dare our employees cheer when thousands of guests have just been disappointed! It was hard to argue with that. While the cheering wasn't malicious, it was clearly shocking and unacceptable to the guests. Backstage sure came onstage that day.

## WHAT'S ONSTAGE IN YOUR ORGANIZATION?

OUR CONVERSATION ON THE PHONE & WRITING EMAILS —

Now let's look at how the onstage/backstage concept can apply to other organizations. For example, what's it like to stay in a nice hotel and see soiled towels spilling over a bin parked in the stairwell? Worse yet, how about walking beside a stack of left-behind room service trays waiting for pickup — and then seeing those same trays sitting there hours later? A common issue with some healthcare facilities is the tendency to leave unsettling materials where patients can see them — materials such as medical tools and supplies, blood, or bio-waste. Staff may even park a very sick patient awaiting treatment in a hallway for all to see instead of taking a bit more time to find a private waiting area.

I once conducted a series of management training sessions for a retail organization in the back offices of their stores around the country. During a break in one seminar, I took a few moments to observe the onstage operation. The store was well designed and the merchandise was nicely displayed. But I noticed something else. Employees had to make frequent trips to the stockroom to retrieve items for their customers. Each time an employee entered the stockroom, he or she would leave the door open to make it easier to carry the merchandise back out. The stockroom looked like any other: boxes were piled high; shelves were crowded; papers and clipboards were everywhere. Not a very attractive sight for any shopper. Once back with the managers in the seminar, I pointed out the problem. One of them argued that the door was only open for a few moments. Yes, I said, but for those few moments, all the hard work that had gone into designing "the show" was compromised. And it happened ten or so times an hour. That's a lot of backstage coming onstage!

Now let's talk about the behavioral side of your business. I find that most companies don't make it a priority to abide by the onstage/backstage philosophy or bother to train employees in appropriate onstage behavior. Think of the car or boat salesman who steps on his cigarette just as you walk up and then shakes your hand with his smoking hand.

Other times, employees are trained but choose to ignore the expectations. How many times, for example, have you felt as a customer that you were an interruption? I remember recently checking into a hotel and waiting while the front desk hostess finished some paperwork. When she saw me waiting I could tell she was annoyed that I was taking her away from her "real" work. Or have you ever walked up to a few employees to ask for help, and they continued their personal conversation as if it were more important than providing good service to you? Almost every time I went into my previous bank (I've since switched), the same two tellers would be talking (usually about a teller who wasn't there).

*WALK w/DECISIVE STEPS*

Without breaking stride and paying no real attention to me, one of them would take my deposit, stamp it, print the receipt, and hand it to me. Such a conversation may seem harmless, but it comes between the show and the customer and may even cause unnecessary resentment. Consider the whispering between a technician and a nurse while you're awaiting lab results or the hushed conversation between a loan officer and mortgage broker when you're waiting on an approval. In this age of technology with so much personal information available online, a simple raised eyebrow or sheepish look between employees who are accessing your file can be disquieting. *INDUCING FEELING OF ANXIETY*

Here's an example of the extreme. A few years ago, I was flying on an airline that was going through a labor dispute. While boarding the plane, I overheard a conversation between a maintenance technician and a flight attendant. The technician was clearly agitated and said to the flight attendant, "I've just had it — I'm quitting. I've gone ahead and put in an application with Delta. I'm just waiting for the results of my psychological test to come back." "*Psychological test?*" I thought. I was hearing this from the technician who had worked on the plane I was boarding. Believe me, I wanted to see the results of that psychological test, too! Of course, that same conversation would have been normal and reasonable if it had taken place out of earshot of passengers. But instead they chose to hold a backstage conversation onstage.

There's not an industry out there that cannot benefit from the onstage/backstage philosophy. Even call centers, where customers never set foot, can gain from this lesson. In that case, when an employee is on the phone with a customer, he or she is onstage, and anything that detracts from that one-on-one conversation is an intrusion and belongs backstage.

There are countless other examples of backstage invasions:

- Unpacked boxes of merchandise crowding store aisles
- Garbage in view (and in whiff) in a restaurant parking lot
- Employees eating or drinking in front of customers
- Employees allowing filing or other work to take precedence over acknowledging customers
- Notes and memos to employees posted in sight of customers
- Employees smoking in sight of customers. (This situation, ironically, is very common in the healthcare industry. You often see hospital employees smoking in a designated smoking area — at the entrance to the hospital!)
- Employees complaining to a customer about another department or employee
- Employees reading newspapers or personal materials while working
- Employees who have the volume of their two-way radios turned so high customers can hear all the operational chatter

I'm sure you can think of your own examples of such irritating interferences. I'm sorry to say, they appear in business all the time, and each time they do a little of that company's hard-earned brand image disappears. Kmart, for example, has been challenged by this image problem in recent years. It has become common to see boxes of stock in the aisles, overhear personal conversations between employees, or face a frowning check-out clerk when one of your items doesn't have a price on it. Their backstage and onstage environments have converged and their business has suffered.

AT THE GROCERY VOUT LINE, SHE SAID HI & CONTINUED HER CONVERSATION W/ANOTHER CHECKER.

## LIVING THE PHILOSOPHY

In my seminars I encourage participants to identify backstage components that pertain to their organization — those physical elements necessary to the operation of the business yet never part of what customers should see. I then ask them to identify back-stage behaviors customers should never witness or overhear. More often than not, participants' responses clearly indicate they know exactly what's appropriate and inappropriate. They seem to really get the onstage/backstage philosophy. But, when I ask the same participants how often that philosophy is violated in their own companies, the answer is usually, "All the time." Why is it that we know the appropriate behaviors yet repeatedly breach the code? Maybe it's just too hard to do it right. Under the pressure of day-to-day work, many employees and managers opt for the easy way out; in other words, they do what's best for them, not what's best for their customers. Consistency comes only when new habits become a way of life, when the philosophy becomes a standard, and when leaders model the onstage/backstage behavior every day, train their people, and reward those who live the concept.

Beyond commitment, separating what goes onstage from what goes backstage takes a certain amount of courage. People at every level need to get comfortable holding each other accountable. Employees need to feel free to say, "That's not how we do things around here." Taking personal responsibility for protecting your organization's brand image may seem like an overly ambitious goal. But with time, practice, and attention, it can become habit.

### *Never Let Backstage Come Onstage*

*IF CHANGES TO STAFF, WHO SHOULD BE ANNOUNCED - FOR IMPROVEMENT*

---

## QUESTIONS FOR APPLYING LESSON 1

1. What makes up the physical backstage of your organization? *MAIL, PHONE CALLs, EMAILs*

2. What makes up the "attitudinal" backstage of your organization? *MAIL, PHONE CALL, EMAILs*

3. What organizational "magic" or "illusion" should not be compromised? *CARE, TIMELINESS*

4. How can you incorporate the onstage/backstage philosophy into your organization's training?

5. What does being "show ready" mean in your operation? *ANSWER THE CALLS ON TIME, START WORKING THE LIST,*

6. How can you ensure that your operation is always show ready for customers? *PRIORITIZING THE WORKLOAD*

\* \* \* \*

# *What Time is the Three O'clock Parade? Is Not a Stupid Question*

### BEHIND THE QUESTION

Besides free access to rides and big paychecks (ha!), one of the real thrills of working at Disney World was watching guests experience the park. Almost daily, I got to see smiling and giggling children nearly float with happiness down Main Street USA. I saw parents acting like children, taking pictures and videos of everything from the castle to a pigeon eating french-fries off their plate. I saw grandparents having more fun than anyone as they rode Cinderella's Carousel, shook hands with Mickey Mouse, and watched their families have the time of their lives. As they say, and as I witnessed, Disney World is the happiest place on earth.

More often than not, Disney World could also be the wackiest place on earth. Where else can you witness grown men wearing green Goofy hats or elbowing their way through a sea of small children to get an autograph and a picture taken with Princess Jasmine? I once watched a couple of nuns in a Tomorrowland Grand Prix Raceway car gleefully slamming it into the car a priest was driving just ahead of them.

I saw plenty of childish behavior and craziness at Disney World, for sure, but most often it manifested itself in what the guests asked. Each one of us as cast members had the same experience: we were stopped and asked humorous questions by guests over and over almost every day. Some of these questions we expected, but others took us by surprise.

Here is a sampling of some of my favorite guest questions:

- "Do you work here?" Asked of me as I stood in front of a fake submarine wearing a Captain Nemo costume.

- "Where is the castle?" The famous edifice was actually within plain sight, looming one hundred and eighty feet over the guest's head.

- "Is Walt Disney really frozen in a special room in the castle?" The frozen Walt rumor was one we heard a lot. (Truth be told, when he died Walt was cremated and his ashes were interred at Forest Lawn Cemetery). But the legend endures. Someone even wrote a book about bringing Walt out of the deep freeze, titled *Waking Walt*.

- "Can you turn off the rain?" Some guests actually thought Disney employees could turn the rain on and off at will. The company was even accused of making it rain to sell more of their famous yellow ponchos.

- "Is that suit air-conditioned?" No. Being a chipmunk was a hot job. Period.

- "If Goofy and Pluto are both dogs, why can Goofy talk and Pluto can't?" There was no good answer for that one — they were just cartoon characters.

- "Are Mickey and Minnie married, dating, or living together?" Usually it was a father who asked this one.

- "What time is the three o'clock parade?" This one was the classic, the all-time favorite wacky Disney World question.

Other questions can't be published here (maybe another book), but the point is, guests could be pretty funny even when they didn't mean to be. And while questions like these amused the other employees and me, they really weren't stupid. Dedicated cast members knew that there was usually a question behind the question. We had been taught that though guests' expressed questions might seem off-the-wall, their intended questions were usually legitimate. For instance, when a guest asked, "What time is the three o'clock parade?" what they really wanted to know was what time the parade got to a particular spot. The parade route, you see, ran all the way down Main Street and beyond, over a mile in distance. So, while the parade started at three o'clock, it arrived in some locations up to thirty minutes later.

When a guest asked a costumed employee, "Do you work here?" what they really wanted was help. When they asked about turning off the rain, guests were typically venting their frustration *EVEN THOUGH* (albeit in a funny way). What they really wanted to know was what they could do while it was raining and when the rain was expected to stop.

As a cast member, I noticed time and time again that guests at Disney World were often completely overwhelmed. For a lot of reasons.

First, the place is pretty big. Think about these Disney World facts:

- The property spans 47,000 acres. That's twice the size of Manhattan.
- It holds four of the largest theme parks in the world all in one place — Magic Kingdom, Epcot, Disney's Hollywood Studios, and Disney's Animal Kingdom.
- There are twenty-nine major hotels on the property.

Second, I witnessed how the place could be a bit frightening. For example, a five-foot tall mouse could be quite scary to a three-foot tall child. Talking trashcans alarmed many guests, and parents constantly worried about the safety of the seatbelts on the roller coasters and keeping up with their kids.

Third, guests were often on SENSATION sensory overload at the park. In most cases, they had saved for years for this vacation and they were going to cram everything they possibly could into the time they had.

In light of these factors, it was easier for me to understand why guests asked what they did and to forgive them for being rude or insistent. Some guests, for instance, swore that the last time they had visited Disney World they had taken a ferry boat from the Magic Kingdom to Epcot. They were upset to find that we had stopped that service. Another guest let me have it one day because he had been told by a friend about the live sharks in the water at 20,000 Leagues Under the Sea, and he had traveled a long way only to discover that they were all fakes. In these cases, and many others, the guests were absolutely one hundred percent incorrect. There was never a ferry running from the Magic Kingdom to Epcot. As a tired and, more often than not, uncomfortably hot employee, I was tempted to put those guests in their place. I came very close to asking my shark friend if he had thought about the fact that no fish could survive in heavily chlorinated and chemically dyed water. But that wasn't the Disney way.

Our stated philosophy was this: our guests may not always be right, but they will always be our guests. One of my Disney colleagues, Jim Cunningham, put it even better when he said, "The guests may not always be right, but let's allow them to be wrong with dignity." Either way, the rule was never to make a guest feel stupid.

## WHAT ARE YOUR CUSTOMERS'
## STUPID (NOT!) QUESTIONS?

During my customer service workshops, I ask participants to share their own examples of unusual customer questions. Everyone has examples and some of their favorites are included in this list:

- "How can I get money out of my computer?" This was asked of a bank teller.

- "Why isn't this computer you sold me working?" This was shouted over the phone at a computer store employee. The employee went to the customer's house only to discover that instead of plugging the computer's power strip into the wall, he had plugged it into itself.

- "How often should I apply this twice-a-week ointment?" The question was asked of a pharmacist.

- "How much do I save with the two-for-one special?" This was asked of a grocer.

- "How many nights do I have to stay to get the free breakfast?" This was asked of a hotel night clerk.

Regardless of role or level, employees can respond to each example in one of two ways. They can respond in a sarcastic and condescending way, or they can listen for the need behind the question, empathize, and answer in a way that preserves the customer's dignity (while still having a secret chuckle). The first approach might make the employee feel superior, but the cuscustomer will most likely feel patronized and embarrassed. The second, kinder approach allows the employee to be truly considerate and leaves the customer feeling grateful.

Unfortunately, some employees have a burning need to feel superior. They resent being in a service role, maybe believing it's beneath them, so they look for opportunities to show who's in charge. This attitude is damaging to customers, businesses, and ultimately the employees who harbor it.

A colleague shared a story about trying to get his car repaired. When he brought his car in, he started to explain the problem to the repair shop service advisor. "Are you a certified technician?" the service guy smugly asked. "No, but I thought my observations might be helpful," offered my colleague. The service advisor replied, "Customer observations waste time." At this, my colleague picked up his keys, backed his car out of the garage, drove off, and never returned.

That service advisor's need to feel superior that day cost the company not just one customer but many. Anyone who heard my colleague's story would probably avoid that garage.

I once observed an embarrassing exchange between a flight attendant and a passenger that illustrates the choice we all have to demonstrate egotism or empathy. This was back in the days when all electronic devices needed to be shut down before takeoff and landing. As the crew was preparing to close the cabin door, the lead flight attendant made the usual announcement to "turn off all personal, portable electronic devices." An elderly gentleman in front of me continued to chat away on his cell phone. The flight attendant, now with irritation in his voice, repeated the announcement to "turn off all personal, portable electronic devices." The man continued to talk on his phone. From the look on the flight attendant's face as he charged down the aisle toward us, I could tell that the wrong choice was about to be made.

"Sir! Did you not hear my request to turn off all personal, portable electronic devices?" All eyes were on this unfortunate passenger. I leaned forward and quietly said, "He wants you to turn off your cell phone." "Oh," he replied, looking humiliated, "why didn't he just say that?" Good question. Most of us don't call our cell phones personal, portable electronic devices. We call them cell phones. The flight attendant could have gently asked the passenger to turn off his phone. But he didn't. Instead he chose to flaunt his authority, use industry jargon, embarrass a passenger, and make everyone else feel uncomfortable. Is it any wonder that airlines are rated extremely low on the customer service scale?

So what does all this mean?

It means that our customers are not stupid. It means if we're going to create or sustain customer loyalty, we have to look at every situation through the eyes of the customer.

## THE EYES (AND EARS) OF THE CUSTOMER

While customers don't always know what we know, the opposite is also true. We certainly don't always know what they know. It pays to listen, and it pays to stop and try to see things the way they see them. When we view situations from customers' perspectives, then and only then can we understand the question behind the question and approach them with respect. When we see things through the eyes of our customers, we can give up the need to be right and allow them to be right instead.

When we listen as customers, we don't hear stupid questions. Instead, as at Disney, we hear excited children, whirring rides, parade music, and energized crowds. We experience guests' bewilderment and excitement. We understand what they really need. And we reply in their language, not our jargon. Most of us have been uncomfortable as customers when an employee answers a question using acronyms and terminology we'd need a company manual to understand. In most cases, the employee isn't using "internal speak" to be rude; more likely the employee has been doing the job for so long she simply thinks everyone else knows what she does. I know. I sometimes accidentally slipped into Disney speak when answering guests' questions.

- "You'll need to take the monorail to the Poly." *Poly* meant *Polynesian Resort*.

- "I'm sorry, Space Mountain is 101." *101* was two-way radio speak for *broken*.

- "I work at 20K." *20k* was our abbreviation for *20,000 Leagues Under the Sea*.

- "The ELP starts at nine o'clock tonight." *ELP* meant *Electric Light Parade*.

Each of these replies left guests more confused than they'd been before they asked their question!

When we look through the eyes of customers, we see lights, colors, spinning rides, and dancing characters. We realize how they may not see the castle in front of them or the obvious sign for the restroom. We empathize. And as we employees empathize with our customers, important changes happen inside us. Our demeanors brighten. The jobs we are doing seem more important to us. We want to help. Most important of all, we never ever need to make a customer feel stupid.

Seeing through another's eye applies to personal relationships as well as business situations. Many years ago my wife Debbie and I were taking our sons, Danny and David, on vacation to California. David, our youngest, was about three years old at the time and, like many small children, he would cry during take off and landing because his ears popped. As we were landing in California he began complaining that his ears hurt. My wife searched through her purse to find some chewing gum for him but only found a bag of M&Ms. Thinking that chewing on an M&M might do the trick, she handed one to him and said, "Here David, this should help." And he promptly stuck the M&M in his ear. That story has been a family favorite ever since. But it is also one more example of how we tend to think everyone knows what we know.

Putting yourself in the customers' shoes is one of the great secrets to creating unforgettable experiences for them and gener-ating positive word of mouth for your business. Companies can implement this concept in many ways. Leaders can train employ-ees to listen for the question behind a customer's question and to demonstrate acute empathy. Company communications, such as newsletters, team meetings, and management updates, should feature stories of employees who delight customers by seeing things the way they do. These employees should be celebrated as role models, their success stories serving as examples for other employees. I can't remember a single issue of Disney World's employee newsletter that didn't have at least one story of a cast member creating a magic moment for a guest by really understanding him or her.

Remember, while customers' funny questions might amuse us as employees, it's our job to amaze the customers by answering ✗ each and every one with grace, compassion, and interest. And as I said, it's OK to laugh — but only on the inside.

### *What Time is the Three O'clock Parade?*
### *Is Not a Stupid Question*

---

#### QUESTIONS FOR APPLYING LESSON 2

1. Describe some of the common yet bizarre customer questions or behaviors that sometimes occur in your business. *THE NSA DOES NOT DO ANYTHING FOR FRIENDS COMING FROM IRAN —*

2. In the circumstances listed in question #1, what is the question behind the question, or the issue behind the issue? *ISSUE BEHIND THE ISSUE*

3. How do employees in your organization respond to "unusual" customer behavior or questions? *I LISTEND & ASK QUESTION TO MAKE SURE*
*(Continued on the next page)* *I AM NOT WRONG*

---

4. What examples of internal speak or jargon should

you avoid when conversing with customers?

5. How can you be sure that your customers who make

a mistake are "wrong with dignity?" *I HEAR THOSE
COMMENTS ALL THE TIME INCLUDING MYSELF.*

6. What processes can you, your work unit, or your

organization implement to better understand the

"lens of the customer?" *To LEARN ABOUT THE ART
OF LISTENING-*

* * * *

## LESSON 3

# *Little Wows Add Up*

### MAKING DREAMS COME TRUE

I saw the whole thing as it occurred. The family of four nearly danced as they walked out of the Main Street USA Ice Cream Parlor, each of their cones piled high with two large scoops. As they strolled along, the youngest child, who couldn't have been more than three, beamed as she licked away at her strawberry ice cream. She was, after all, in a place where dreams come true, enjoying the most delicious dessert imaginable.

Suddenly, though, the ice cream slid off her cone and hit Main Street with a big, pink splat. I watched as the little girl's lower lip quivered. She froze in her spot. Her brother pointed and laughed. Her mother and father reached down to console her. And the little girl, who moments before had been the happiest child on earth, burst into tears.

I was ready. As a Disney employee, I had been trained to see this as a rescue opportunity, a chance to turn a tragic moment into a magic moment. I quickly approached the family, dropped to one knee, and smiled as I reassured the little girl that these things happened all the time. And then I asked, "Do you still want strawberry?" The tears suddenly stopped, and the girl nodded. Her mother smiled in surprise and appreciation. When I returned with a fresh strawberry cone, a custodial cast member was already mopping up the spilled ice cream, telling the child, "It's okay, it happens all the time. That's why we have mops!"

In a few minutes the girl was beaming again, and the family found a table so they could sit down and carefully enjoy their ice cream. They were happy: I was happy.

For us as cast members, moments like these made all of the hard work worthwhile. They kept us going. The realization that we had the privilege to create special memories for other people was empowering. When we needed to recharge, we knew all we had to do was look for opportunities to wow a guest. And there were plenty of chances at Disney World to do just that. To put this in context, Disney's research estimated that guests come in contact with between sixty and seventy cast members each day they are on the property. So, Disney made it a big part of our jobs to connect with the guests, to wow them in small ways whenever we could. Here are some examples:

- A cast member at Disney's Animal Kingdom would take a snapshot of an entire family so that the family's designated photographer could appear in at least one picture. (Or of the honeymoon couple. . . *together*!)

- Another cast member would pick up on the lost look on guests' faces and offer help. *we pick up the tone of voice,*

- An Epcot security host would hand out an "official" citation to a young guest for having the biggest smile of the day.

- A horticulture host would invite an interested elderly guest to help him plant the last flower.

- Snow White would call your child by name (by secretly reading the name that was stitched on the back of your child's Mickey Mouse ears).

- A Main Street USA supervisor would replace a child's dropped ice cream cone.

While these examples represent genuine acts of kindness, they don't necessarily knock your socks off. But the magic of these little wows is that they added up. Small, yet sincere personalized actions, as they accumulated, had a tremendous impact on guests at Disney World. And when these wowed guests left, they couldn't wait to come back.

## WHAT WOWS ARE YOU CREATING?

When I talk about this concept with my audiences, almost everyone has a great example of a little wow that left a big impression:

- A drycleaner put a pin left on a jacket lapel in a separate plastic bag to protect it.

- A drive-through bank teller sent back hard candy for the kid and a dog biscuit for the pup!

- The coffee server you see every morning greeted you by name and asked if you wanted the regular.

- The retail clerk carried out your packages, thanked you, and invited you back.

- The mechanic who replaced your tire also cleaned your wheels.

- The doctor, not appearing to be rushed, sat down and encouraged you to ask questions before your medical test.

ASK FRIENDS To CALL ME DIRECTLY IF THEY ANY Qs–

No matter what business you're in, every employee at every level has numerous chances to wow customers. You just need to be on the lookout for chances to amaze.

RESPOND To PERSONAL EMAILS w/THANKS–

Here's an example of a series of little wows that added up for me. Unpacking in a Chicago hotel the evening before I was to conduct a speech, I realized I had forgotten to pack a pair of dress shoes to wear with my suit. The hotel's concierge suggested a store called the Walking Company in a nearby mall. When I arrived, the store was so crowded I considered leaving. But one of the salespeople made eye contact with me. It wasn't the kind of eye contact that said, "Oh no, another customer." Instead, it was a friendly look that said, "I know you're there, please don't leave, I'll be right with you." Wow!

Feeling good about having been acknowledged, I browsed around for a couple of minutes and found a pair of shoes I liked. Only moments later, the salesperson approached me and said,

"Sorry about the wait, let's get you some shoes." I showed her the pair I was interested in and asked to try a size ten. She said, "Let's measure your foot just to make sure." I know I wear a size ten, but her whole demeanor showed that she wanted to make sure I got the right shoes. Wow! *RELATING TO*

She measured my foot and said, "Size ten is right, but you have a very Rubenesque foot." "Rubin, who?" I thought. I didn't know whether to be offended or proud, as I had absolutely no clue what she meant. "I've got to tell you," she began, "the type of shoe you've selected won't be the most comfortable for you. I think this other style would feel much better." Being the skeptic I am, I looked at the price of her suggested shoes to see how much she was upselling me. Same price. Hmm. With nothing to lose, I tried on the style she suggested, and the shoes fit extremely well. To this day, they are still the most comfortable pair of shoes I've ever owned. Wow!

One of my favorite Orlando restaurants is Seasons 52. The first time my wife and I ate there, the experience was truly wonderful. The food was delicious, and our server was impressive with his knowledge and attentiveness. We couldn't wait to go back. When we did, we were again wowed in many small ways. Our server was just as professional and knowledgeable as the one we had had before. He recommended a great bottle of wine and even gave us the chef's recipe for a favorite dish. Now we're regular customers. I can't say the staff tops itself each time we dine there, yet little wows continue to show up in new ways. For example, the restaurant's linen napkins are traditionally black, but one evening my wife came in wearing a nice white skirt, and our server imme-diately offered her a white cloth napkin to avoid the risk of dark lint showing up on her skirt. Because we have consistently been treated with care at Seasons 52, because we are made to feel we matter there, because we are wowed in small ways each time we go, we are faithful and happy customers. The real wow has become that they are consistently excellent.

Sometimes my clients express concern about wows becoming the standard over time. They believe if you continue to go above and beyond each time, that's what customers will come to expect as normal service. They're right. And that's a good thing. It keeps you and your employees constantly looking for ways to improve. And when you have reached the point where customers, because of their interactions with your company, expect wow service — like my wife and I do at Seasons 52 — then you have succeeded in creating a supreme differentiator and extreme loyalty.

## THE HOW BEHIND THE WOW

Many business books discuss what's commonly known as the Wow Factor. But like my dubious clients, readers (and many employees) are often skeptical about repeatedly wowing customers. Why is this so? I believe, in general, it may be because customer expecta-tions are on the rise, and it gets more and more difficult to please, let alone amaze people. Maybe it's those of us who write business books who are to blame. We love to tell grand stories — stories about employees going way above and beyond to astound a cus-

*WALK SLOWING*

tomer. We feature big wows like the store clerk who trudged through a blinding snowstorm to bring groceries to an elderly customer. And there is the famous account of a Nordstrom's employee who refunded a customer's money for a returned set of tires, even though Nordstrom's doesn't sell tires.

Such tales are remarkable, but most employees are usually too busy to leave the checkout line to trek through the snow to deliver groceries. Or it's not in their union contract to go outside during poor weather conditions. Most employees today don't have the authority to take returns for merchandise they don't even sell. They're thinking, "Take a set of tires back? I can't even take a tie back without my manager's approval." As a result, stories like these, meant to inspire, only frustrate and discourage employees.

So, while the big wows are wonderful, it's more effective to start with what one client calls "wee wows" — the little things that make customers think, "That was nice." Smiling, calling a customer by name, and paying attention to his or her children are all examples of little wows. As I said before, individually these actions are no big deal. But, again, the secret is this: small wows add up.

So, how can your organization regularly create little wows for customers? In the course of working day in and day out with a lot of pressures, how can employees take the time to consistently deliver the little extras? And how do leaders make sure everyone sees the importance of delighting their customers? I believe it involves three steps — what I call the beyond strategies.

### Step 1: Wow Through Know-How

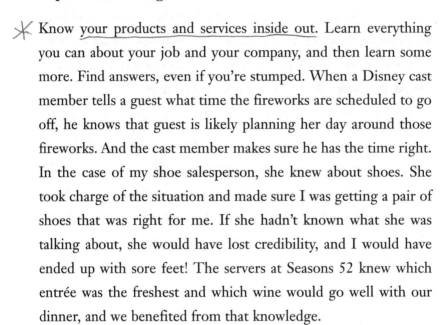

Know your products and services inside out. Learn everything you can about your job and your company, and then learn some more. Find answers, even if you're stumped. When a Disney cast member tells a guest what time the fireworks are scheduled to go off, he knows that guest is likely planning her day around those fireworks. And the cast member makes sure he has the time right. In the case of my shoe salesperson, she knew about shoes. She took charge of the situation and made sure I was getting a pair of shoes that was right for me. If she hadn't known what she was talking about, she would have lost credibility, and I would have ended up with sore feet! The servers at Seasons 52 knew which entrée was the freshest and which wine would go well with our dinner, and we benefited from that knowledge.

### Step 2: Take Notice; Take Action

Look for ways to help. Acknowledge customers, don't delay, and don't ignore problems. Return calls and emails quickly. Seek out customer contact rather than waiting for customers to come to you. Don't pretend you didn't see the child drop her ice cream cone. You can't wow a customer unless you first notice him. Then, of course, you should act.

### Step 3: Add Flair through Care

Do your job with enthusiasm and compassion. When the cast member took a photo of a family so that everyone could appear in the picture, she was demonstrating that she cared about that family's experience. My Walking Company salesperson could have easily brought me the pair of shoes I originally asked for. But she wasn't selling shoes; she was selling shoes that were right for me. There's a big difference — a difference that says, "I care." One might argue that such a level of care takes too long. But it only took a few extra moments for the salesperson to measure my foot and to check my type of foot (Rubenesque!). Her care actually saved time. Rather than having to bring out two or three pairs for me to try, she only had to bring out one pair — the right one. Don't focus on conducting transactions; instead build relationships. Amaze the customer by sincerely caring.

Another way to Add Flair through Care is to have the mindset that customers should be better off because of their interaction with you. For example, I often suggested that Disney guests view the parade in Frontierland, even though that was at the end of the route, because I knew it would be less crowded there with better picture taking opportunities. Guests really appreciated knowing this. I left the Walking Company with more knowledge than I had when I came in. I now know to ask for extra arch support in my shoes.

Consider some of your best service experiences — the server who made the perfect dinner recommendation, the computer help desk employee who gave you a tip on how to make an application more effective, or the clothing store employee who helped you coordinate colors. I'll bet in most cases of outstanding service, you learned something.

These three simple strategies, followed consistently, will allow you to create your own wows. Applied, they turned me into a loyal Walking Company customer and a Seasons 52 frequent diner. These techniques can benefit any job in any industry, and they make the difference between mediocre service and outstanding service. It doesn't matter if you're an electrical engineer with an aerospace company or a taxi driver; these strategies work. The main thing is to look for opportunities to offer the little wows.

When a company prepares and encourages employees to follow this game plan, not only are customers wowed, but employees feel good about themselves, knowing they're making a difference. Think of a company you are truly loyal to - not a company that holds you captive because of your frequent buyer benefits, but one that you patronize over and over because their people really do provide a great experience. Chances are you revere that brand because, in addition to a great product, the employees are knowledgeable, responsive, and caring. And every once in a while they may even teach you something. Wow!

### Little Wows Add Up

RAISING THE BAR

## **QUESTIONS FOR APPLYING LESSON 3**

1. What are some examples of occurrences that have caused one of your customers to literally exclaim, "Wow!"?

2. What are some examples of simple courtesies that prompt smiles and gratitude from your customers?

3. What actions can you take that demonstrate you truly care about the customer's experience with your organization?

4. What behaviors demonstrate excellent responsiveness? TIMELY RESPONSE & COMPERHENSIVE INFORMATION

5. What opportunities are there to teach customers something they may not have known before? EXPLAINING RULES & WHY THE RULES PLACED FOR THE SITUATION* * * *

# *Have Fun With the Job — No Matter How Miserable You Feel*

The day I was transferred from 20,000 Leagues Under the Sea will stay with me forever. Not because I had a sentimental connection to a submarine that didn't actually go under water or a real fondness for fake fish. Truth is, I welcomed a change, and Disney was pretty good about giving cast members a variety of experiences. Frequent transfers not only kept things interesting for the cast members, they also helped schedulers maximize labor flexibility. The more attractions cast members could work, the easier it was to place them where they were needed the most.

No, the reason I vividly remember my transfer was not due to what I left behind, rather it was what lay ahead. I was moved to

37

It's A Small World. Now just the mention of that ride's name sends shudders up most adults' spines, right? So you can understand how hearing that song eight hours a day, five days a week was sheer torture. Well, I lived that nightmare for about eight months, and to this day, I can't walk by the ride without a twitch.

Guests often gush to cast members, "How fun it must be to work at Disney World." Yes, of course it was fun; it's the happiest place on earth, right? But it was also tiresome (listening to that song over and over), uncomfortable (ninety-five degree temperatures with ninety-five percent humidity), humbling (wearing turquoise polyester and striped suspenders), and monotonous (repeating, "Watch your head and step," again and again). Sometimes it was all a cast member could do to keep from screaming, "I can't take it anymore!"

So, what kept us going?

We knew that our jobs and our attitudes about our jobs were vital to the guest experience. Our principle role was to create happiness and magic, and that responsibility had to trump any frustrations we felt. Knowing this, we cast members endured the heat, suffered through the sameness, smiled, and acted happy. Usually when we did this something wonderful happened to us. Just by acting happy, we became happy, and (tah-dah) the job became fun (most of the time).

How can you have fun while suffering the humidity and heat, endless questions from guests, and repetitive duties? By creating it. Talking with guests, joking with them, learning where they were from, commenting on what was printed on their t-shirts, and trying a thousand other little tricks all made the job fun or, at the very least, bearable.

Before you start thinking how like Pollyanna I sound, let me point out that there were plenty of times my boredom and frustration showed through. Seeing the dark side of things sometimes is, after all, human nature. We all tend to focus on the negatives, lose sight of the big picture, and forget to appreciate that we are blessed to have a job. When I became sick of it all, sometimes a fellow cast member would bring me back to the bright side, or a manager would, in no uncertain terms, remind me that I was being paid to delight our guests. Worst of all were the times a guest would say something like, "Smile, it can't be that bad." Sometimes I wanted to shout back, "Oh yeah? Why don't you try wearing this ridiculous outfit and listening to that damn song all day!" But usually a guest comment like that would jolt me back to my responsibilities. People were spending huge amounts of money for this Disney vacation, and there I was bumming them out. To recover from my wallowing, I would usually joke with the guest who made the comment, snap out of my funk, and do my job. I would say something like this: "I was just thinking I need to pick up a recording of this song so I can listen to it at home." The guest and I would both chuckle, and that was that.

While working at It's a Small World may seem like the most unpopular job at Disney World, there was one that was actually worse. That was being the poor schmuck they stuck in front of Space Mountain when it was closed for maintenance. I know. I had to do it now and then. Sometimes, you could explain to disappointed guests that the problem was minor and the ride would open later in the day. Other times, however, the ride was closed for a major overhaul. I then had to tell guests the bad news: it wouldn't open for another two months. Oh, boy. Upon hearing that, some guests would completely melt down. "We drove all the way from Seattle (always far away places) just to ride Space Mountain," they would cry. "Thanks for ruining our vacation!"

Feeling like Ebenezer Scrooge, I would think, "Hey, come on! It's not my fault, and besides, there are like a million other things to do here!" But Space Mountain was the most popular ride in the park and guests were understandably upset when it was closed. But having them blame me for something out of my control, and worse, having them blame me for ruining their vacation was a tough thing. How could anyone find fun in that situation?

It was a challenge, but the secret again was to look for the fun. OK, don't roll your eyes, stay with me here. If you look hard enough, fun can be found buried in just about any job. The whiners don't even bother to look, but employees who care about what they do can uncover it.

My goal in tough situations like manning a closed Space Mountain was to make guests smile. I was careful not to trivialize their anger or frustration, but I knew if I got them to smile I would earn my pay for the day and could put a check mark in the win column. I wasn't always successful, but I usually was. Sometimes it was a matter of explaining to a guest that work was being done to make the ride even better than before, throwing in some cool trivia such as the fact that Space Mountain is actually the tallest "mountain" in Florida. Or I'd share a secret about what was being upgraded. Getting the inside scoop as a guest was a bonus worth smiling about. I would also tell them that if they were to come back in the future, they could find me, and I'd personally escort them to the front of the Space Mountain line. While they knew this was a bit over the top, it usually got a little smile. And no, no one ever took me up on the offer.

Other times, simply empathizing with the guests worked. I would let them know how badly I felt about the ride being closed. It was always an amusing irony when a guest would smile and reply: "It's okay; it's not your fault. I guess now we have a reason to come back."

There were a few times, though, when I could tell by the passion or hostility in guests' reactions on hearing the bad news that a vacation or their emotional well-being was really in jeopardy. While those responses were rare, they did happen. As soon as a guest appeared to be borderline hysterical, I'd quickly ask, "What rides haven't you been on yet?" Hurriedly focusing on the closest one mentioned, I'd encourage them to go directly to that ride, and I would arrange for them to bypass the line (a quick phone call was all it took). This offer always got a smile — and sometimes even a handshake and a hug, too.

Was it possible to make my job fun each and every moment of every day? Of course not. Sometimes the only thing that kept me going was the anticipation of my upcoming break. I'd think, if I can just survive another hour I could go get a soda and complain about my supervisor for awhile. Most of the time, though, I was able to find enjoyment for both myself and the guests - even if it was a small thing like teasing a child by suggesting their recently purchased stuffed Pluto was barking, sneaking an elderly guest's hat off his head, or asking a family to name each of the Seven Dwarfs (Sleepy, Sneezy, Doc, Dopey, Happy, Bashful, and Grumpy).

## FUN CAN BE HARD TO FIND/THERE'S A SMALL WORLD EVERYWHERE

In my seminars, participants often challenge me about how easy it must have been to find fun in my job at Disney World. "That's a magic kingdom where fun's the name of the game," they say. "Try making my job fun."

Working in a credit collections department, for instance, must be a stressful and often unpleasant job. After all, a collections agent's job is to call people who can't or won't pay their bills and get them to pay. When is a phone call from a bill collector fun to receive? Well, try being the one calling. Sometimes collections agents are verbally abused or physically threatened for having the nerve to ask for money that's owed. Collections agents have to make such calls all day long. Some agents, of course, can't take the emotional turmoil and make a career change. Others, however, excel at the job, love what they do, and have no desire to ever leave the department.

No, they're not Sopranos-like mobsters who enjoy threatening to break debtors' thumbs. While they take no pleasure in another person's misfortune, successful collectors have mastered the art of making their job fun. They know that very few debtors are credit criminals who never intend to pay. Sometimes, bills or checks do get lost in the mail. In most cases, people who owe have either overextended themselves or gone through a traumatic event such as a divorce or the loss of a job. They're usually embarrassed by their inability to pay and are under great stress. Good collectors understand this. That's called empathy, and it's very important in customer service. OK, but where's the fun?

Effective collectors see their work as a challenge. They're energized by the prospect of helping a customer get out of a hole while at the same time making sure the money is paid. The mission, therefore, is not simply to get the money. They also want to keep the customer. I've done several training programs for collections department leaders (there's an association for everything!), and I always ask how many of them have collectors who regularly receive thank-you notes from customers. Believe it or not, almost every hand goes up. Agents who receive thank-you letters are the ones who get charged up by helping people, procuring the money, and keeping the customer. And is it any coincidence that these are also the agents who can view their work as, well maybe not a barrel of laughs, but as a positive thing?

Of course, collections agents aren't the only people who have trouble finding fun in their work. Those who perceive their jobs to be mundane or unimportant also face difficulties enjoying work. Here's an example that had a significant impact on me. One time in San Francisco, just hours before I was to make a speech ~~scuffed~~ SCRATCHED for a bankers' convention, I noticed my shoes were scuffed up. I didn't want to go onstage with scuffed-up shoes, so I sought out the shoeshine stand in the hotel lobby. Operating a shoeshine stand is a potentially mundane job. But it sure wasn't for this operator. Once I was in the chair, he asked me when my shoes had last been shined. He said there was some polish buildup he needed to remove and went at it, showing me how buildup caused dullness. I saw exactly what he was talking about, and I was actually engaged in what he was doing.

He commented on the excellent quality of leather used for my brand of shoes, which made me feel pretty good, and he recommended ways to keep the leather supple. He asked if I found the shoes to be comfortable, and when I admitted I did, he mentioned other brands that had a similar fit. All the while this shoeshine operator was giving my shoes a workout like they'd never seen. When I got out of the chair, my shoes sparkled, and I knew how to keep them that way. I'm pretty frugal, but I think I tipped him fifty percent for that shine. Why? Because it was the best shoeshine experience I'd ever had.

The way he made his job fun was to be an expert. He didn't make idle chit-chat. He educated me. He impressed me by treating my shoes as prized possessions to be cared for and looked after. He clearly has fun doing his job and probably makes a very good living doing it.

Making the mundane pleasurable is a real skill, and it's all about attitude. Of course, we've all seen the flip side of this same coin — employees who are absolutely miserable in their jobs and make sure everyone knows it. Such employees rarely look for the fun, and if they ever do it's often at the expense of customers or other employees. Some clear signs that an employee has lost or never found the fun include the following examples:

- They don't make eye contact when you, the customer, approach. They see you as an interruption. You don't exist until they look up from what they're doing.
- They recite their spiels *PHRASE* in a robotic manner. The words might be right, but there's no sincerity in them. The employee is simply regurgitating a script. *REPEATING without COMPREHENDING*
- They recite the above script in a monotone voice.
- They blame another person or department for a problem the customer might be experiencing. "Yeah, we've got a bunch of new people back there. They don't know what they're doing."
- They use off-putting body language such as turning their backs toward you or frowning as they wait on you.
- Their facial expressions signify boredom.
- They use "they" instead of "we" when referring to their own company, suggesting a detachment from that company or job.

As a customer, you probably see these behaviors every day as you interact with employees of various companies. You may continue to do business with such a company as long as it's conve-

nient, but you aren't really loyal. When something better comes along you're likely to bolt.

So, how about your company? Are your employees having any fun with customers and their jobs? Are you? Work is certainly not recreation or sport, but if you're going to spend half of your waking hours at it, shouldn't you at least have a little fun? If I were to look into your eyes as you do your work, what would I see? Would I see the eyes of someone who enjoys what they do or would I see the eyes of someone who has lost the joy?

## FINDING THE FUN IN YOUR JOB

Here are eight tips for creating fun on the job:

1. **Smile**. When you smile, even when you have to force yourself to do it, you somehow engage positive emotions within, and things actually begin to brighten.

2. **Play with customers.** I'm not saying be silly or disrespectful. I'm saying let them know you're happy to see them or to be talking with them on the phone. Let your personality shine through and get customers to think, "I'll bet that would be a fun person to know."

3. **Connect with co-workers.** Some can be a curse on our work lives, but others can be beacons of light when we're having a tough day. You know who lifts your spirits. Engage with those individuals.

4. **Don't take yourself too seriously.** Look at your work through playful eyes and discover the humor all around you.

5. **Bear in mind you're paid to have fun.** Your boss or the board of directors may not agree with this idea, but I'll be happy to argue the point with them. Employees who enjoy what they do are far more likely to do their job well and to satisfy customers than those employees who see work as drudgery. → HARD, DULL WORK

6. **Fake it.** What would someone having fun at your job look like, act like, or talk like? Look, act, and talk like that, and you'll be amazed at how quickly your attitude improves.

7. **Make a contest of it.** How many customers can you get to smile in an hour? How many defect-free widgets can you produce today? How many teaching moments can you create for customers today?

8. **Remember the greater good of your job.** At Disney World, our purpose was to create happiness. If you work for a law firm, your goal may be to bring clients peace of mind. If you work for a bank, your mission may be to help customers achieve their financial dreams. A job's purpose is always bigger than a job's tasks. Taking reservations at a travel agency is more than booking trips – it's giving people an experience they'll never forget or uniting families. Reconnecting with your job's purpose is a great way to find the job's fun.

If you absolutely, positively cannot find the fun in your job then do yourself a huge favor. Find another one. I can think of few things more depressing than people who spend their whole lives doing work they absolutely despise. And let's face it; doing a good job is nearly impossible if you find no delight at all in your work. If you've irreparably lost the joy in your work, you owe it to yourself, the organization, and the customers to look for something else.  IN A WAY THAT IT IS IMPOSSIBLE

We all know that work cannot and should not be a laugh-a-minute playground. But you can still have fun even during trying moments by applying these tips. And those moments when you want to throw your hands in the air and scream are precisely the moments you need to step back and look for the fun. While you may have to look pretty hard, pleasure can prevail.

### *Have Fun With the Job — No Matter How Miserable You Feel*

## QUESTIONS FOR APPLYING LESSON 4

1. What are some of the stressful or unpleasant *HEARING UNFAIR JUDGEMENTS ABOUT THE ORGANIZA-TION* aspects about your job or some of the jobs in your

   organization (your "Space Mountain is closed" *HAVE* situations)? *TELLING THE FRIENDS THEY HAVE TO WAIT LONGER TO GET THIER ID CARD -*

2. What are some ideas for finding the fun in those *IT IS MORE FINDING RELIEF THAN FUN! I DON'T KNOW HOW?* situations, while being respectful of customers?

   *SAY PRAYERS FOR THEM*

   (Review the eight Finding Fun In Your Job tips) *INNER TRANQUALITY*

3. Within reason, what does having fun with the job

   look like and sound like in your role? *ENJOY DOING WHAT I DO -*

4. How does your organization promote fun for

   employees? *OUR WORK IS NOT Vd ON ALL THE TIME, WE ARE TRUSTED TO ASK Qs IF SOMETHING IS NOT CLEAR TO US.*

5. What can be done to raise the fun factor in your

   organization? *HR COULD HAVE A LUNCH & LAUGH DAY / PER WEEK AS OPEN MIC -*

* * * *

# Don't Be a Customer Service Robot

### ANIMATED SERVICE

My friend and colleague, Barbara Farfan, was making some adjustments to the queue at Disney-MGM Studio's (now called Disney's Hollywood Studios) Muppet Vision 3-D attraction. Line management was a regular part of Barbara's job as an attraction hostess. A situation required her to direct the waiting guests down another aisle of the queue. "Step this way, folks. Step this way. All the way to the end, all the way to the end," she said as she waved them in the direction she wanted them to go. Line 'em up, move 'em out, get the job done.

But this particular time as the guests followed her orders, one of them started to moo…like a cow. "Moo…Mooooo," he bellowed. Others caught on and quickly joined in the mooing as they moseyed cattle-like to the other side. They probably figured if they were going to be treated like cattle, they might as well act (and sound) like cattle. Even though Barbara burst out laughing with the guests, she admitted later that she had been pretty embarrassed. How many other times, she wondered, had she treated guests like livestock? It was a powerful wake-up call.

This chapter is a natural follow up to the previous chapter, Have Fun With the Job — No Matter How Miserable You Might Feel, because it further explores a major challenge for companies and employees: the banal and repetitive tasks that are a part of nearly every job. In the previous chapter, I focused on how to make such work fun for ourselves as employees. In this chapter, I'm focusing on ways to make these experiences more fun for customers.

Consider the Jungle Cruise skippers in the Magic Kingdom. Their job is to recite a script while taking guests down the "Amazon River," often twenty times a day, five days a week. The ride is as old as the Magic Kingdom itself, yet it continues to be a favorite for millions of guests. How is this so? I think it's because when these skippers pretend to steer the boat (it's mechanical), they also steer just a little bit off the script to keep from sounding mechanical. Here's how it works. Once the Jungle Cruise skippers have the script memorized, they are encouraged to tweak it to fit their personalities or the situation. While they need to stay close to the storyline so that each guest gets a consistent experience, they add their own bits of humor, irony, and mischief. "Skipper

Dave will help you out of the boat by the rear. Not that rear, ma'am; this is Adventureland, not Fantasyland." Over the years a few of the "improvisations" crossed the line of G-rated Disney appropriateness and had to be dropped. But more often than not, the improvisations make the ride a thrilling and fun adventure for each and every guest. These Jungle Cruise skippers are some of my favorite cast members at Disney because they've mastered the art of making the routine appear fresh and spontaneous.

"Watch your head and step," was a phrase I must've recited thousands of times during my career as a Disney ride operator. And, I admit, over time I just repeated it in the same dull, robotic manner. But then one day, a guest pointed out it was physically impossible to watch one's own head. True. And, yes, the comment was delivered sarcastically. But like Barbara's "moo-moment," it made me think about what I was saying and stopped me from giving another robotic performance.

Although a task may be second nature to us, we can't afford to have it look or sound mechanical to our customers. A key principle in customer service is to be fully present and never simply go through the motions. We must make them feel like valued people, certainly not like cattle.

## ROBOTS ROAM THE PLANET

Examples of robotic customer service are everywhere, in all industries. How do you feel when you receive a scripted sales call? "Hello, Mr. Snow, how are you today? That's great, Mr. Snow.

The reason I'm calling is…" How interested in you is that person on the other end of the line? Sometimes my first thought is that it's a recording (and it sometimes is).

Disney World used to offer a training class called "Put a Smile In Your Voice." The purpose of the class was to train employees who worked on the phone to sound authentic, happy, and willing to help. The class taught cast members to put a face to the voice on the other end of the line and avoid mechanical responses. A few years later, Disney made a decision to have all telephone operators and reservationists end every phone conversation with the statement, "Have a magical day!" The intent was to add a bit of pixie dust to the phone interaction. The risk in asking employees to deliver such a phrase was that if it were said in a monotone voice, it would sound ludicrous. And it surely wouldn't be very magical.

When customers encounter robotic employees they end up feeling processed. They don't feel appreciated. Here are a few examples of robotic behavior:

- A bank loan officer instructs her customer to sign here, here, and here, without acknowledging that the customer is using the money to send her only child to college.

- A nurse says, "You're my 9 a.m. blood draw," and sees the patient as only an arm.

- A preacher shakes a congregant's hand and tells her how nice it is to see her as he looks over her shoulder to the next person in line.

- A server asks, "How's the burger?" but leaves before he gets a response.

- A receptionist hands a patient a clipboard and eight forms to fill out without speaking or looking up.

- The server ambles over to the table, hands the patrons a menu, then walks away without a word.

- The mail carrier forces an envelope clearly marked Do Not Bend into someone's mailbox.

Unfortunately, the longer employees are in their jobs, the easier it is for them to fall into this kind of wooden, indifferent behavior. What happens is that they begin to take their customers for granted and treat them as tasks instead of people.

The easiest trap to fall into is being mechanical with the words we use as we go about routine duties. Consider the following phrases when said in a robotic or indifferent way:

- "Have a nice day." This phrase is often said as an employee is turning to the customer behind you, forgetting your existence. When said in this way what the employee really means is that he's done with you, you're dismissed. Don't you think if he really wanted you to have a nice day, he would have looked at you and smiled as he said that?

  *IMPATIENT, ANNOYING*

- "Please hold." Those are two of the most infuriating words ever spoken over a telephone, always followed by the click of the hold button. Why even say please? Much better to ask, "May I put you on hold for a moment?" and then wait for a response. Ninety-nine percent of callers will say it's OK to put them on hold, and those who say no either have an urgent situation or have already been given the runaround and need someone's attention.

- "How are you?" or "How 'ya doin'?" When an employee says this in a monotone voice with no eye contact, you can be pretty sure he could not care less how you are. Try answering with a real explanation of how you feel and watch the confused look come over that employee's face.

- "Next." As you wait in line for whatever it is you're waiting for, you are called forward with that weary expression. If there is one word that should be purged from every employee's vocabulary it is "next." Did you ever see the Soup Nazi episode of Seinfeld? That's what "next" feels like. You feel like a nobody. A simple, "I can help you now, sir," or "Thank you for waiting," accomplishes the same thing as "next" but in a much more respectful way.

After reading a touching story about "Johnny the Bagger" by Barbara Glanz, I was reminded of the time I observed a group of grocery store baggers as I waited in the checkout line. The line was pretty long so I had some time to really observe — a much better use of my time than leafing through the tabloid magazines and, it turns out, much more entertaining. The sackers were all working hard, grabbing items as they were scanned, putting them in bags, and placing the bags in a cart. Over and over again. Most of the baggers, while efficient, worked in an impersonal, robotic way. There was no interaction with customers other than a curt, *BLUNT, SHORT*

"Have a nice day," as they started bagging the next person's groceries. These baggers saw their jobs as tasks.

Two baggers, however, took a different approach. As they sacked groceries they spoke with the customers, joked with their kids, and made comments like, "I love this kind of ice cream." They worked just as quickly as the other baggers, but the effect was very different. These two employees didn't make customers feel like tasks, they made customers feel noticed and important. I'll bet those two baggers also enjoyed their jobs a whole lot more than the other sackers, and I'll also bet they're going to be successful at whatever they do in their future careers. They took care and pride and put effort into their jobs to make the mundane magical.

And how about Southwest Airlines? The company has experienced years of profitability when most airlines are struggling to survive. In addition to low fares, on-time departures, and one of the best luggage handling records in the industry, Southwest is also known for jazzed-up safety spiels delivered by the flight attendants. On most other airlines the flight attendants recite (or read) a script as quickly as they can with little or no vocal inflection or sense of care. Usually the spiel sounds robotic, and in fact many airlines now simply turn on a tape with a recorded message. Hey, if it sounds recorded anyway why not just use a tape?

Southwest flight attendants, on the other hand, make the spiel fun. They deliver those necessary but boring safety instructions in a variety of creative ways — as songs, raps, or poems. They poke gentle fun at the idea of an airline passenger in this day and age needing to be told how to operate a seatbelt. After explaining that adults should put on their own oxygen masks before assisting a child, they've been known to add "or anyone acting like a child." The flight attendants have turned a routine responsibility into a fun, engaging performance. And guess what? Passengers actually listen. And, what's more, they really like it. Being on an airplane that's circling an airport, unable to land due to weather issues, is not a lot of fun. But again, I've been on Southwest planes where flight attendants did what they could to *make* it fun. I've seen them lead trivia games and even hold singing contests. I'd still prefer to land (when it's safe), but I appreciate the efforts of those flight attendants.

## BE ANIMATED, NOT AUTOMATED

How can you turn your mundane into magic? While it takes some thought and a strong commitment to the customer experience, those who put in the effort stand out from the pack. Think about the most routine elements of your job in which a customer is involved. How would a robot handle the interaction? What would a robot do and say during the transaction? Do an honest assessment of your own and your organization's approach to customers. Is your treatment animated or automated?

So, how can you become more animated? What is the secret to avoiding the trap of robotic behavior? First, think about routine duties as a part of the overall customer experience and treat those tasks with the same care and focus you do with other more specialized tasks. The customer doesn't care if you've waited on fifty other people that day, cashed three hundred checks, or loaded two thousand other guests into rocket vehicles at Space Mountain that hour. Treat each customer as the only one and as an interesting, dignified person. View each interaction as a chance to connect with another person. The idea is simple, but it works.

After a speech in which I discussed the idea of moving from a task mentality to a people mentality, a participant approached and asked if we could talk for a few minutes. She said she was a payroll clerk for a large company and loved what she did. Her job was to meet with newly hired employees and have them sign volumes of paperwork for tax withholdings, automatic deposits, benefits choices, and so on. She said most of the other clerks saw the work as merely a task to be completed and treated new employees in just such a manner. "Welcome aboard, now sign these." New employees, and she couldn't blame them, complained of feeling processed.

She went on to say that she considered herself to be a good-will ambassador for the company. She explained: "I'm the first person a new employee meets. I set the tone for everything else, and I take that very seriously. I remember how nervous and overwhelmed I was on my first day of work, and I want our new people to know that I'm glad they're here, I care and am there to help whenever they have any questions."

She went on to tell me she had recently been on medical leave. With her eyes full of tears, she talked about the many cards and letters she had received from people whose first day of work she had impacted. Her story was so moving. Here was someone who had made a routine task memorable.

As you look for ways to improve customer service on a regular basis, it's important to acknowledge that certain duties are more likely to result in robotic behavior than others. These are usually the tasks we do repeatedly, often hundreds of times a day. Here's a list of examples:

- Answering the telephone
- Ending a telephone call
- Taking up cash, tickets or boarding passes
- Responding to email
- Taking a customer's order in person or over the phone
- Taking a phone message
- Leaving a phone message
- Answering a customer's question
- Having a customer fill out routine paperwork
- Checking a customer in or out

Each of these duties has the potential to become either task oriented or people oriented, either automated or animated. Consider taking tickets. As guests entered any Disney park, a cast member would take and tear the stub from their ticket. (They now use advanced technology, but the cast members are still there.) For years these cast members were called Ticket Takers, and guess what they did? They took tickets. Then, someone had the simple but insightful idea to change the title from Ticket Taker to Greeter. This change of title changed mindset and performance. The cast members still took tickets (or passed them through a scanner), but they understood their actual job was to make guests feel welcome at Disney World. It was no longer just a task but an important job.

I read somewhere about a company who changed their receptionist's title to Vice President of First Impressions. How is that for inspiring and impacting behavior? The point here isn't to go around changing everyone's title. The point is to see beyond the task to what is really important to customers. They want good service, but they also want to be treated as human beings who matter.

### *Don't Be a Customer Service Robot*

---

## QUESTIONS FOR APPLYING LESSON 5

1. As a customer, what are some examples of robotic service you have received?

2. How did you feel about your experience when you received robotic service? *I WISH I DID NOT HAVE TO HEAR IT*

3. Are employees in your organization ever guilty of providing robotic service? How do you know? *ASKING CUSTOMERS TO FILL OUT FORMS*

4. In your job, what routine tasks could potentially appear robotic to customers – with the result that they feel they've simply been processed? *SAME*

5. What can be done to personalize the tasks listed in question #4? *I DON'T KNOW!*

6. How can you make what is automated in your organization (such as voicemail, phone trees, or Web site) more "animated"? *NEW VOICE MAIL PROCESS*

\* \* \* \*

# *Pay Attention to the Details — Everything Speaks*

## DISNEY DETAILS SPEAK

In today's world, theme parks are everywhere — especially in America. Some of these parks are worth the price of admission, and some are not. Some are cheap attempts to put on a show, offering little more than typical fairground rides, a few arcade games, cotton candy, and homemade fudge. They get by because they call themselves *"Something-or-other World."* But they probably don't get by very well. Others are magnificent places, adventurous and safe, with literally hundreds of millions of dollars invested in every little detail of storyline and quality.

The classic, in fact the first of the breed, the park that is credited with launching the theme park industry, is Disneyland. It is the park that launched the entire modern-day theme park industry. But more important than that, it is still the standard by which all other theme parks are judged.

SUITABLE

Aptly enough, it all began with an inspiration. When Walt Disney's two daughters were children, he often took them to amusement parks and carnivals in the Los Angeles area. As he sat watching them go around and around on the carousels, he began imagining what his own amusement park would be like. In his mind, it would be a place where parents and children could have fun together, a place where families could have an experience like no other, a place where safety and care were the rule. It would be spotless and well maintained, he mused. Instead of surly, unkempt workers, his employees would be friendly and well groomed. Instead of "paying customers" (or suckers), his patrons would be known as "guests." Instead of scattered rides and random rows of games and junk food, his park would be carefully laid out so that people could easily find their way around. At his park, there would be magic at every corner.

You know the rest of the story. Walt Disney's dream, of course, became reality.

So, you may ask, what is the secret to such success? How were Walt Disney's ideas transformed into actuality so beautifully and so meticulously? And how are these standards met again and again, year after year, at Disney parks? The answer is pretty simple: attention to detail. Let me give you an example. When Walt

Disney designed his theme parks, he not only laid them out in a cohesive and sensible way, he also divided them into different "lands." At Disneyland, guests walk through Adventureland, Fantasyland, Frontierland, Tomorrowland, and Main Street USA. In Walt's mind, these lands weren't to be just catchy names. They were to be "authentic" interpretations of a specific era and location; and that's what they still are. Main Street USA, for example, takes guests back to the early 1900's. Everything there — everything guests see, hear, smell and taste — enhances that nostalgic experience. Guests ride on a steam train or in horse-drawn carriages; they hear a barbershop quartet; they smell and taste the freshly popped popcorn; they sit on old fashioned benches in Town Square. In fact, the only thing modern on Main Street is the guests' attire.

At Epcot's Universe of Energy Pavilion, Disney's Imagineers (the engineers responsible for designing new rides and attractions) recreated the smells of a pre-historic, primordial swamp in the dinosaur scene. How they knew what a pre-historic, primordial swamp smelled like, I don't know, but details like that transport guests to a world millions of years past. People literally get lost in the Disney details. And that's the idea; that's where the magic is.

When I was at Disney World, such fanatical attention to detail was evident everywhere. It didn't stop with design. For instance, we cast members understood we were a key part of the lands and rides we represented. We knew we had a responsibility to maintain the attraction's integrity by paying attention to the details.

We wore appropriate costumes and played our roles with enthusiasm. We picked up that stray piece of trash. We reported the peeling paint on the fence. We made sure the stockroom door was closed so guests couldn't see backstage.

On the other hand, some examples of attention to detail might seem a bit odd or over the top. The horse drawn trolleys traveling up and down Main Street USA add to the early 1900s atmosphere. But imagine if one of those horses died right there on the street. Well, we had a "dead horse procedure." I won't get into specifics, but it involved a big tarp, a forklift, and ultimately a chainsaw. As far as I know, performing this procedure has never been required. And just so you know, we should all live the life those Disney horses live. They're treated like equestrian royalty.

I call this idea of extreme attention to detail "everything speaks." It means that every detail of an operation, down to the smallest cobweb (whether intentional or not... *think Haunted Mansion!*), says something about that organization. Each Disney employee was trained to get into the habit of asking this important question many times a day, "Are the details around me saying what they should say?" Because, whether we want it to or not, everything speaks.

## WHO ELSE IS SPEAKING
## AND WHAT ARE THEY SAYING?

Regardless of the business or industry, employees send hundreds of messages each time they interact with customers. Even if your business is virtual, your website speaks volumes. In that case, how easy or difficult it is to navigate and get information communicates a lot about your brand and makes a huge impression.

Sometimes these messages are trivial such as a napkin stain or withering flowers in a flower bed. But sometimes they can be significant like an unattended help desk or dangerous potholes in the parking lot. Trivial or significant, every detail says something about the organization's brand.

Here's a pretty potent example of the everything speaks philosophy. A friend told me about taking her husband to an out patient facility for minor surgery. While she was sitting in the waiting room, she noticed a beautiful, large aquarium and walked over to take a closer look. Guess what was floating on top of the aquarium? A dead fish. What do you think this detail said to my friend as her husband was undergoing surgery? "They can't even take care of the fish here!" I know this seems like a ridiculous leap of logic, but I also know that reason sometimes has nothing to do with what goes on in a customer's mind. What about the tray table that won't fold down properly on an airplane? "How's that engine running?" What about the dental office with the rusty water fountain? "How clean is that drill?"

Customers are almost always aware of the everything speaks idea. Whether we think so or not, they notice things. Cheap plastic chairs offered to customers to use as they fill out paperwork for a $500,000 mortgage, filthy restrooms in a posh restaurant, or rickety shopping carts in the grocery store parking lot all tell a powerful story. And examples like these can significantly diminish a company's brand.

Consider these other examples:

- A pretty pricey hotel I once stayed in had a sign taped on the bathroom mirror that read: "Towels are inventoried every day. Guests will be charged for any missing towels." What did the sign really say to hotel guests? Most likely something like, "You are probably a thief, so don't even think about taking our towels." While the management didn't mean to send that message that is what was implied. Because everything speaks.

- A colleague spent several thousand dollars to have some legal documents drawn up by a well-known law firm. As she reviewed the documents she saw that everything was in order except three things: her name, her company's name, and the date. She'd just spent thousands of dollars on what turned out to be boiler-plate documents on which the attorney didn't even bother to fill in the new client's information. My friend felt cheated, the law firm was embarrassed, and they lost a client forever.

- I was once waiting on my car to be serviced. In the customer waiting area, there was a sign over the coffee machine that read, "We return your car clean." When I went to help myself to a complimentary cup of coffee, I noticed that this area of the room was really dirty. The table had what looked like two years of ring stains on it. How's that for irony?

- I was boarding a small commuter airplane in Abilene, Texas. As I walked up the steps to get onto the plane, I noticed a frightening detail; there was duct tape on the leading edge of the wing (I took a photo to prove it). Although I'm a big believer in duct tape, this was pushing it a bit too far. I said to the pilot as I walked past him, "There's duct tape on the wing!" It turns out it was actually what's called high speed aviation tape. You know what? I don't care what it's called. You are certainly not sending a comforting message when passengers clearly see you've repaired an aircraft's wing with tape — any kind of tape.

- A friend was taking her mother for dialysis at a local healthcare clinic. In the waiting room, she looked around and saw several dead or dying plants. What message of care did that send? Not a good omen. Everything speaks.

These examples demonstrate how fragile a brand can be. Any disconnect, such as tape on an airplane's wing, causes customers to doubt the company's promise. An airline's promise is to get you to your destination safely. A law firm's promise is to understand your needs and provide peace of mind. A premium hotel's promise is to make you feel like a welcome guest, not a thief. And a healthcare center is meant to promote health, not death! In each of those cases, the company's actions canceled out their promises.

On the other hand, you can always tell when an organization does embrace the everything speaks philosophy. They may not call it that, but they clearly get the concept. Everything just feels right and there's a reassuring consistency. The result is trust. Here are a few examples:

- In the dental office, the cleaning instruments are carefully laid out before you arrive, your last x-ray is already on the light panel, and your chart is on the counter, ready and waiting. Everything communicates preparation and attention to detail.

- The appliance repairman shows up at your house in a clean truck and an immaculate uniform, with the proper tools and paperwork. Everything says that he is a professional and knows what he's doing.

- The coffee shop has clean tables and floors, a well-stocked condiment station, and an organized serving location. Everything communicates care and quality.

I recently visited one of the engine plants owned by Cummins. The plant produces over two hundred diesel engines per day and is an amazing operation to observe. The most astonishing thing to me, however, was how clean and organized everything was when I visited. Remember, this is a diesel engine factory! Cummins allows potential customers (often large truck manufacturers) to regularly tour the factory as part of their relationship-building process. When these customers see the care and attention to detail that go into everything there, the sale is pretty much a done deal. After all, these customers reason, if Cummins puts that much effort into maintaining immaculate facilities, they must pay at least as much, if not more, attention to building excellent engines.

## WHAT'S "BEING SPOKEN" IN YOUR ORGANIZATION?

Examine your own workplace or even your workspace with an everything speaks mindset. Are the details consistent with your organization's brand promise? Do the details communicate a positive message? The right message? Put everything to the test, and go with your gut reactions as they are likely to be accurate. Better yet, take trusted customers on a walk through your facility to get their perspectives. Tell them to not hold back — to give you honest, unedited feedback. Tell them what image you are trying to create, and ask what they might see, hear, touch, taste, or smell that adds to or detracts from that image. Whatever you do, don't justify the problems your customers point out. Accept the feedback and ask for more. You can decide later if and how you will take action.

I'm not suggesting that you abandon good business sense as you consider and improve your environment. Attention to detail doesn't have to be expensive. A Disney myth, for example, is that the hitching posts on Main Street USA are painted every night whether they need painting or not. The theory being that such attention to detail communicates a powerful commitment to quality. The reality is that doing such unnecessary work would communicate a willingness to waste time and money. The reality is that the hitching posts are painted when they need painting.

A comment I often hear in my business leader seminars is, "I'm too busy to see these details." Remember, the key here is commitment. Make noticing things (and doing something about it) part of your daily routine. If you have to meet with a colleague from another area, take the long way to his or her office and look at what speaks along the way. When you're coaching an employee, if appropriate, take a walk while you're talking and look at the messages that are being sent all around you. Engage the employee in the same process. Front-line employees often tell me, "I really don't see the little details," or "Expecting me to notice such small problems is unrealistic." Besides, many of us think that if we don't notice certain details, then the customers surely won't. Wrong. They do notice. Again, everything speaks.

The owner of a large truck stop ran into this response from his employees. During one of his employee meetings, he encouraged them to help keep the place looking good by reporting maintenance problems and picking up any litter they saw. He got the standard arguments: "I'm too busy to see it," and "It's not my job." So, before the next team meeting he conducted a little experiment. He scattered a few crumpled up dollar bills around the facility and observed employees as they picked up every dollar. When he called them on it during the next meeting, they had no choice but to admit it was all a matter of motivation.

Motivation works, but so does pride — pride in the job you do and the brand you represent. Whether you are a leader or a front-line employee, if you really believe that everything speaks and you are proud of your job and company, you'll find a way to take care of the place. And, interestingly, the more you take care of the place, the more pride you'll have in it. Employees are naturally proud of a well-designed, well-maintained workplace and most will do their best to ensure ongoing quality and attention to detail.

Implementing the everything speaks philosophy has an interesting and surprising side benefit. Customers will actually help. Disney World guests, for example, are an important part of the company's custodial team. Because the place is so clean, most guests feel too guilty to throw litter on the ground. On several occasions I saw a guest chastising another for carelessly discarding a popcorn box or a soft-drink cup. If a customer is loyal to a brand, they want to help in upholding that brand's impeccable image. And as mentioned, they are the best interpreters of the idea that everything speaks. Where this philosophy is valued and implemented, everyone — managers, employees and customers — cares about preserving the quality of the brand.

### *Pay Attention to the Details — Everything Speaks*

---

## QUESTIONS FOR APPLYING LESSON 6

1. How does the Everything Speaks philosophy apply to your job or organization?

2. Take a walk through the physical environment of your organization (preferably with a team or even a customer). What messages are being "spoken" in your work setting?

3. What needs to happen in order to ensure the details support your organization's brand?

4. How can you and your organization implement or increase commitment to the Everything Speaks philosophy? *BRING UP POINTS FOR IMPROVEMENT*

5. How does the Everything Speaks philosophy apply to your organization's *backstage* environment? What messages are being communicated to employees? *TRAINING WE ARE DOING ON REGULAR BASES,*

*SENSE OF BELONGING*

* * * *

# Never Ever Say "That's Not My Job" — Don't Even Think It

## BEHIND THE PRIDE

We were gathering for our weekly management staff meeting. In those days the whole management team could fit in one conference room. Bob, the Vice President of Operations, came to the front of the room to start the meeting. Bob could be pretty intimidating, and the look on his face showed he was anything but happy. We all braced ourselves.

"I was walking through the park this morning after opening," he began, "I saw that one of the backstage gates had been left open and guests had a clear view backstage." Oh, oh. But he wasn't finished. "So, of course, I closed it. I saw a supervisor in the area and mentioned that the gate had been left open and was disappointed he hadn't seen and taken care of it." But that wasn't the bad part. "So, the supervisor says to me, 'I did see it, but I'm not a supervisor in that area.'"

*RETURNING AN ITEM IN CARLSTON'S*

There was a collective gasp from the assembled group. This was the supreme Disney sin. From the day a cast member joined the Disney company, it was clear that saying anything remotely close to, "That's not my job," was about the worst thing he or she could do. That supervisor might just as well have walked up to Bob and said, "Bob, I would like my career here to be over." I doubt he lost his job that day, but I'll bet he never made the same mistake again.

I believe that one of the reasons Disney has been so successful is that they make it a priority to cultivate a strong sense of ownership in their employees. Cast members treat the guests and the facilities with genuine care, concern, and pride. You know the sense of ownership you feel when you buy a new car? The care with which you treat it (at least for a while)? That sense of ownership is what Disney tries to instill in each cast member.

*ACHIEVEMENT w/COURAGE*

Over the years, I was able to observe many of the ways they achieved this remarkable feat. Hiring to this strength was certainly the first step. Disney made a point of selecting people who demonstrated personal accountability. Beyond hiring, they continuously reinforced the importance of our having pride in the company and the jobs we did. At Disney World, employee ownership was sought, taught, and expected every single day. It was non-negotiable.

Ask most people what they do for a living and they usually respond by telling you their profession: "I'm an engineer." Or they may also tell you where: "I'm a mechanic for Ford." Compare these responses to those given by Disney cast members. More often than not they simply say, "I work at Disney World." They may offer more, but only if asked. It's a subtle contrast, but it's significant. You see, my colleagues identified more strongly with the company than with their individual jobs. They were proud to work for Disney. And that pride allowed them to develop and demonstrate ownership. CARE, PRIDE, SHARE w/OTHERS

PREVILAGE VS ENTITLEMENT

So how did this pride and ownership play out on a daily basis at Disney? How did personal accountability impact the brand image? When I ask people what impressed them most about their visits to Disney World, invariably the first response is how clean they found the park. People are always amazed at how a place so big could stay so clean. Well, it's not so amazing when you realize that every single one of the 60,000 or so cast members was expected to help keep it clean. It gets back to never saying, "It's not my job."

ETHICAL IDEA

So how did the company get all of those people to pitch in? I mentioned pride. Well, Disney had a phenomenal way of connecting with and building on the cast's sense of pride. But where did it come from? Some people describe Disney employee pride as built in. Sure, the Disney brand has enjoyed a long-standing positive image of excellence. This might explain how the pride was originally instilled. But how, decade after decade, has it been

EXPLANATION AND GIVING OPTION IS VERY IMPORTANT

fostered? How have notions like never saying, "It's not my job," been programmed into cast members' brains?

The Disney culture includes a lot of legends, and an important part of any leader's job is to recount those stories to inspire and sustain the company's traditions of excellence. Dick Nunis, former Chairman of Walt Disney Attractions, used to regale the opening crews of new rides, lands, or parks with stories of the challenges of opening Disneyland and Disney World. How "everyone did everything," titles didn't matter, and how sometimes the paint was still drying as the first guests entered the park, but through hard work and teamwork they were able to pull it off.

The role of a Disney leader also entailed giving cast members new and continuous reasons to be proud of their contributions and recognizing them for their efforts. Formal awards, anniversary celebrations, special events, and daily appreciation reinforced employees' self-respect. Guest letters acknowledging cast members' above-and-beyond service were shared and posted. Team meetings devoted time to celebrating magic moments created by cast members. Plaques, certificates of gratitude for a job well done, and commemorative photos decked the walls. Cast members wore pins marking years of service, special achievements, and even their home towns — all sending the message that they could and should own their jobs and be proud of their work.

But, let's get back to how the company got everyone to keep the place clean. Pride in the brand was certainly key. But there was a more direct reason: we were supposed to pick up trash. It didn't matter if you were Captain Nemo or the Vice President of

Marketing, if you were observed overlooking trash on the ground or ignoring a cluttered guest area, you were coached — that is to say, gently reprimanded. Bob, the vice president mentioned at this chapter's beginning, did a lot of coaching, and many of the other leaders back in the day were comparably strict.

While I know cast members would sometimes violate this rule (and every other lesson in this book), most of us did pick up that left-behind piece of trash most of the time. Occasionally, I was in a hurry and wanted to ignore that empty soda cup or candy wrapper as I passed by. But the guilt factor would surface, and I'd inevitably trace back, reach down, and pick up the garbage. Guilt, I discovered over time, was actually pride in disguise. When it kicked in, it was fairly clear that some inner value was at play — a value that had been instilled by the company and nurtured by what I call the corporate soul. It went well beyond following the rules. In the Disney culture, that inner value was ownership. It was a sense of ownership that made us pick up trash even when no one was looking. It was ingrained. (Even now, I catch myself picking up trash in the mall or in the Starbuck's parking lot. I'm forever embarrassing my kids.) So, when you have 60,000 people devoted to picking up trash, maybe even fanatical about it, there's really no mystery in how the place stayed so clean.

*HIDDEN GEMS*

Early Disney research revealed that the cast members' ability to answer guests' questions was a big factor in guest satisfaction. Employee knowledge thus became a priority at Disney, and a lot of training time was dedicated to teaching cast members everything there was to know about their area of the park or their ride so they could answer questions such as, "How fast does it go?" or "How many fat grams?" or "What kind of fertilizer do you use?" This was more evidence of Disney's commitment to the ownership philosophy. They wanted and expected each cast member to take responsibility for educating and dazzling guests.

But what if someone asked you a question about something outside of your job area? Let me tell you, at Disney, the answer, "I don't know," was a very close cousin to, "It's not my job." I will always remember the day I learned this lesson the hard way. I was working on Dumbo's Flight (one of my parents' prouder moments), and a guest asked me a question about the ride. Without really thinking I simply replied, "I don't know." Well, the guy just lit into me! "How old are you?" he shouted. "I'm twenty," I quietly replied, hoping my voice would calm him. "Well, if you don't want to still be working at Dumbo's Flight when you're forty, never say, 'I don't know' again. You find out!" I was thoroughly humiliated, but since then I don't think I have ever said, "I don't know," without adding, "but let me find out."

The expectation at Disney was that you would find the answer to any guest's question by calling the appropriate area, a supervisor, or the designated information hotline. (Four phone digits could get you to a 24/7 resource that had access to every imaginable bit of information in the "world," whether it was the names of Cinderella's mice, the start time of a show, or the cost of a boat rental.) I was once asked how many bricks there are in Cinderella's Castle. Good thing I didn't make up a number because I called the hotline and found out there aren't any bricks in the castle. It's made of fiberglass.

## WHOSE JOB IS IT IN YOUR ORGANIZATION?

Now let's look at how the ownership concept can apply to other organizations. What's it like to ask a server in a restaurant for water and hear, "This is not my table," or be told by a nurse in a hospital, "I don't work this floor." Or have a post office employee, after you've been waiting in line for an hour, tell you, "I'll need to get the supervisor."

I want to be sensible about this principle: everyone can't do everyone else's job. It's unrealistic to expect a bank teller to repair a leak in the lobby ceiling. It's certainly impractical to expect a hospital housekeeper to adjust a patient's IV tube. As a customer or a patient, I know I don't want that. But, if a teller notices stains or moisture on the ceiling, it should be that teller's responsibility to let someone know. If a patient tells a housekeeper that her IV tube is uncomfortable, it should be that housekeeper's duty to alert a nurse. And it should be the nurse's job to positively respond to that housekeeper. It's supposed to be one organization so shouldn't everyone act like it? Ownership should be everyone's job.

Here's a shining example of the ownership concept. I had been away from home for about a week conducting training programs in several cities. I was to fly from St. Louis to my home in Orlando, spend a day there, then fly out the following day for another series of engagements. On the Sunday I was scheduled to fly home, a major storm was coming through central Florida, and my flight from St. Louis to Orlando was canceled. The airline representative said it was unlikely I would be able to fly that day. Instead of going home for a day and being able to pack clean clothes for my next round of seminars, I now had to travel directly to my next engagement.

So, I extended my stay at the hotel and called to arrange for laundry service. The concierge informed me that the laundry is closed on Sundays, but I could have my clothes cleaned Monday. I told her that wouldn't work because I had to leave first thing Monday morning. She then called the housekeeping department to see what they could do and was informed that no one there even had a key to open the laundry facility. As I considered either buying some new clothes or washing my dirty clothes in the bathroom sink, the concierge said she had an idea and would call me right back. When she called back a few minutes later she said, "Good news! One of our front desk employees is getting off his shift and said if you'll put your clothes in a bag he'll take them home and wash them. And since he lives close by, he'll bring the clothes back tonight." And that is exactly what happened. Thank you, Renaissance Hotel, St. Louis!

There are two heroes in this story. Certainly the employee who cleaned my clothes demonstrated outstanding ownership — truly above and beyond the call of duty. But the concierge was also exemplary. Rather than leave me to my own devices, she searched for a way to help me. She could have simply left it at, "The laundry's closed," and perhaps apologized for the inconvenience. (It wasn't her job to clean clothes.) But that's not what she chose to do. She took it upon herself to solve my problem. While she didn't actually wash my clothes, she saw to it that they got washed. The lesson at hand is not about doing everything: it's about making sure things get done.

A colleague of mine told me about her experience with a sales associate for Irving Oil. She had run out of gas on I-95 and had walked a mile in a blustery and cold wind to the nearest exit where she found a gas station and a kindhearted sales associate. Not only did that associate gladly fill her gas can, he also gave her a cup of coffee and drove her back to her car where he filled the tank with enough gas for her to get back on the road. Where do you think she stopped to top off her tank? It wasn't this fellow's actual call of duty to go the extra mile (literally!), but pride in his job and company and genuine care for the customer created this exceptional moment of service and a customer for life.

In contrast, here is an example of the opposite — the absence of ownership and care. Meet Jim, the music store employee. I had purchased an electric guitar and brought it back to the store to ask some questions about adjusting the strings. Jim gave me some brief instructions, and I asked if he minded making the adjustments for me so that I could see how it was done. His exact words were, "They don't pay me enough to do that."

This employee may have been having a bad day, but I doubt it. His whole demeanor communicated that doing the absolute minimum was his standard mode of operation. He exhibited neither pride in his work nor ownership in his company.

This lack of ownership can cause all kinds of problems for companies and customers. How do you feel when you call a company with a fairly simple question, and you get transferred from department to department because you haven't yet connected with the person whose job it is to help you? As the customer, you have to repeat your problem each time you're transferred. When employees don't take ownership, customers often feel like they are dealing with totally different companies when interacting with different departments. And that frustrates them.

I know some readers are thinking, "Well, in our company we've outsourced some jobs so customers sometimes have to deal with employees who aren't part of our company." It doesn't matter. Customers want to feel like they are dealing with one organization and don't care how your company is structured.

It may surprise you to know that many Disney cast members are not Disney employees at all. The people who sell balloons, operate some of the merchandise locations, and work in some of the restaurants are actually employed by other companies, usually the sponsors of the locations. But the guests shouldn't know that. Even though employed by outside companies, these "cast members" attend the same orientation and customer training and follow the same guidelines and standards as every "real" cast member.

There are many other examples of employees displaying lack of ownership:

- The receptionist who says you'll have to call back and ask the schedulers to change your appointment time.

- The hotel employee you ask for directions who tells you that he's on a break.

- The contact center representative who informs you, "I'm not allowed to do that without a supervisor's signature."

- The employee who responds to your dissatisfaction about something with, "Hey, I only work here."

- The flight attendant who tells you where to look for a blanket instead of finding one for you.

- One of your IT department employees who says: "I can only do what appears on my work request. If you want something else done you have to submit another trouble ticket."

You can probably think of your own examples of being told, "That's not my job," or maybe, "I don't know." It happens more than it should, and when it does it's a clear indication that the organization is missing that main ingredient called employee ownership. The Challenger Space Shuttle disaster was just such an example. Lots of employees apparently knew there were problems, but the culture encouraged them to keep quiet. No one took ownership, and the results were tragic.

## GOING THE EXTRA MILE

In my seminars, I encourage participants to identify what it means to go above and beyond. It's easy for most to describe how this notion translates in their business, and they share countless stories of how they or their employees wow customers on a daily basis. But they also share the common struggle of getting all of their employees to want to go the distance and the struggle of then getting them to do it consistently. The excuse employees use is that things get busy, and it's impossible to do something extra every time. Yet, as with all of these lessons, when a company puts a stake in the ground on what's expected and the leaders model that behavior and link it to employee pride and recognition, that expectation or value can become second nature for everyone.

Being your best and doing your best is not always easy. If it were, everyone would be the best, and no one company would ever stand out in its industry. But we all know that certain companies and certain employees do stand out. They outshine the competition because they are willing to go the extra mile. And going the distance is more than doing just enough. It requires a sense of ownership and responsibility. It requires commitment to doing whatever it takes to do a job well, no matter what job that is.

There is a special energy in a company where employees feel a sense of ownership. You can see the pride in their faces, and you can feel the care in their actions. Customers reward that attitude with loyalty.

*Never Ever Say, "That's Not My Job." Don't Even Think It!*

ABDU'L-BAHA SAY THE SERVICE W/A PREVILEGE BACK W/A PREVILEGE IS NOT OUR, WE ARE GNING BACK

## QUESTIONS FOR APPLYING LESSON 7

1. What are some examples of the "it's not my job syndrome" you've experienced in your organization?

2. What causes that attitude? *Not HAPPY w/THEIR JOB.*

3. How does the "It's not my job" attitude impact your customers? *THEY ARE UNHAPPY & WE LOSE A CUSTOMER. LOSING TRUST, BAD IMAGE,*

4. What are some examples of behaviors that would communicate a sense of ownership to your customers?

5. What can your organization do to ensure that all employees demonstrate a sense of ownership? *SOME TYPE OF CHECK AND BALANCE,*

* * * *

*ONE – ON – ONE w/STAFF IS Good EXAMPLE*

## L E S S O N   8

# *Everyone Has a Customer*

### CAST MEMBERS ARE TREATED THE WAY THEY ARE EXPECTED TO TREAT THE GUESTS

After I had worked at Disney World for a couple of years, I was promoted to my first management position, Supervisor of Fantasyland. By far, this was the point in my life when I was carrying the best business card ever. When people asked me what I did for a living, with the utmost pride and integrity, I was entitled to claim, "I'm the Supervisor of Fantasyland!" It was great in bars.

A few weeks into the job I faced my first tough task: I had to reprimand a cast member. I admit scolding someone is far better than getting scolded, but I was still pretty apprehensive. The cast member was habitually late for work, which caused a lot of headaches for his fellow cast members. At that time, the discipline procedure for an attendance problem at Disney was this: first, two verbal reprimands; second, a written reprimand; finally, job termination. This cast member was on his second verbal reprimand. As I sat in my office anxiously awaiting his arrival and planning what to say, Bruce, my manager, wandered in and sat down across from me. He noticed the cast member's attendance record in front of me. "Getting ready for your first reprimand?" he asked. "Yep," I said, "my first, his second. And I'm going to let him have it!"

Although he knew I was kidding, Bruce said something I've never forgotten: "Dennis, whatever discipline you have to give, whether it be a simple reminder, a reprimand, or even a termination, when the person walks out the door I expect you to make sure he walks out with his dignity."

Wow! What a great lesson for me, and what a great principle for a company focused on service and excellence. No matter the situation, preserve the other person's dignity.

I still had to give the reprimand, but because of Bruce's remark I adjusted my approach. I realized that how I handled the situation was ultimately going to impact the cast member's job performance, and more importantly, his self-respect. I heeded Bruce's advice. I was firm and direct, but I did not "let him have it" or belittle him. If I had, he might have taken that experience onstage, and it could have impacted the guests. After all, it's hard to smile, be friendly, and deliver magic if you've been read the riot act or worse, humiliated. In the end, the cast member knew it was a serious state of affairs, but he left the room whole.

*To TREAT THEM THE WAY (You want To BE TREATED) —*

Disney's philosophy was (and is) this: cast members are treated the way they are expected to treat the guests. This philosophy is right on. I have yet to see a company provide consistently great service to external customers when their internal customer service stinks. Disney's philosophy was not limited to managers. It applied to all cast members. Why? Only half of them worked onstage in direct contact with paying guests. The rest worked backstage in costuming, maintenance, finance, marketing, training, and countless other departments where they interacted primarily with other cast members. But the attitude of these backstage employees who served the employees who served the guests was the beginning of the chain of magical moments.

Let me illustrate this point. If you worked in the Magic Kingdom, here's how you would begin your day. You would park in the cast member parking lot about a half mile from the Magic Kingdom. You would show your Disney ID to a security host and board the shuttle bus that would take you to the main tunnel entrance. If you were early enough, you might have time to grab a bite to eat in the employee cafeteria. You'd then make your way to the Costuming Department, get your costume, and change in the locker room. After clocking in, you would go to your work location, check-in with the supervisor, and get to work.

From the time you parked your car until you reached your work location, you would have had the chance to interact with at least six other employees: the security host or hostess, the bus driver, the cafeteria server, the cashier, the costuming host or hostess, and the supervisor. Each interaction could either positively or negatively impact your day. And if these were mostly negative interactions, the one who might end up on the short end of the deal was the guest.

I know, I know — I said earlier in the book that cast members were supposed to leave troubles or disagreements backstage, have fun with the job, and treat the guests well no matter what. And that was all true. But it only worked if everyone in the company, on or off the stage, believed in treating each other well. If there were just a few isolated times when things didn't go so well, cast members were indeed expected to be professional and suck it up. But if the system broke down regularly, if cast members treated each other poorly most of the time, the guest experience would surely suffer.

Disney backstage cast members went through exactly the same training as the onstage cast. They learned the same service principles, had the same appearance guidelines, and were expected to be part of the show. Most of the time that worked.

Here's a great example. My wife, Debbie, began her Disney career in 1976 as a costuming hostess. At her checkout counter, cast members would tell Debbie their sizes, and she would gather all the pieces of their costumes (shirt, suspenders, hat, belt, bloomers, spats, etc.) and hand them over.

In the spirit of good customer service, Debbie challenged herself to remember the costume sizes of various cast members. When she saw those employees approaching, she would get their costumes (in the right size) before they even asked for them.

Debbie even began memorizing the shifts cast members worked so she could have their outfits ready and waiting for them.

Debbie admits she was especially attentive to the Jungle Cruise skippers, an all-male operation in those days. Even now, over four decades later, she'll see a former Jungle Cruise skipper from back then and say to him, "Thirty-two inch waist, thirty-two inch length, medium shirt." This never fails to completely blow him away because it was exactly the size he wore (not anymore!). These cast members were Debbie's guests, and she treated them like guests.

In the service industry, there's an ongoing debate about internal and external customers. Some believe there are only external customers. Everyone else is just an employee expected to do a job. I disagree. In too many organizations employees start out working on the front lines with external customers, then when they move into internal roles, their attitude changes. It's as if they think, "I'm glad I don't have to work with customers anymore." Well, they do work with customers: their customers are other employees.

## EVERYONE IS (AND YES, HAS) A CUSTOMER

Examples of the misguided perception that employees are not customers are everywhere. Here are some that seminar participants have shared:

- An office worker's computer crashed. We all know how that can bring work to an immediate stop. She called her company's IT department to see if someone could come right away to fix it, knowing the problem was probably due to her error. But she was unprepared for what happened next. When the technician arrived, the employee explained what she had done just before her computer crashed. The tech gave her an irritated look, plopped down in her chair, and started working on the problem, ignoring her. Figuring she was no longer needed, the employee went down the hall to do some other work. When she returned to her desk the technician was gone and her computer screen was "live." She sat down with relief but saw a sign the tech had left on her keyboard. It read: "Intel Inside — Idiot Outside." Now, I'm sure some of you are thinking, "Where can I get a copy of that sign," but think about the impact it had on this employee. How would you like to be the next customer she spoke to on the phone?

- A manager transferred to a new department. During his first meeting with employees, he told them that things were going to be different around there. He felt the previous manager had been too easy on them, and he was going to make some changes. Things went from bad to worse, but the final straw was a poster the new manager hung behind his desk showing a mean-looking gorilla with a caption stating, "If I want your opinion I'll beat it out of you." How'd you like to approach that boss with your million-dollar idea?

- A company was implementing a new benefits package. The changes were significant and the company's employees had a lot of questions. The program participant who shared this story told me she had emailed a benefits question to a Human Resources representative and received an automatic reply that said, "I'm on vacation until July 31st and incoming emails are automatically deleted. If you truly need me, email me again when I return on July 31st." How's that for internal service? No options, no automatic forwarding to someone who *can* help — nothing.

- A hardware sales person was in a client meeting, the deal was about to close, and the prospect asked a question about the product that the sales person couldn't answer. So, the sales person called headquarters, got connected to a Product Specialist, asked the question, and got this response, "That information has been on our website under the product feature tab for two years; you should be able to look it up from anywhere." Click.

How would you feel as an employee on the receiving end of any of these scenarios? My guess is you wouldn't have a warm, fuzzy, "we're all in this together" feeling. More likely you'd be pretty ticked off. And what if this were the norm in the organization? I sure wouldn't want to be one of that organization's customers.

On the positive side of things, Cummins, the diesel engine manufacturer and distributor, has an interesting way of handling the internal/external customer dilemma. They expect everyone in the company to have what they call a "clear line of sight" of the chain leading to the external customer. Meaning, the external customer is acknowledged as the reason for the company's existence, and all decisions must be made with that customer in mind. At Cummins, as in any organization, throughout the chain, there are links where employees support each other in order to support the customer. Distributors, for example, deal directly with customers. The factory workers, having a clear line of sight to the end (the external customers) know their success is based on how well they set up distributors (the internal customers) for success. A distributor may want to provide excellent service in repairing a customer's engine, but if the right part isn't available or the factory is slow in response, he is set up for failure. Cummins is so committed to the process that they rolled out a worldwide initiative called Customer Support Excellence to ensure everyone knows their connection to external customers and how to set their internal customers up for success.

I was once asked by a large company to give a keynote speech at the launch of their customer service initiative. Several times before the event, I tried to contact the company's president to discuss my presentation. I could never get through to him on the phone, and he never returned my calls. The morning of the event the company president arrived just before everything was to start. I asked how things were going and he said, "Things would be going a whole lot better if I didn't have to waste my time on things like this." He walked up on the stage and gave one of the most insincere, uninspiring speeches I'd ever heard. If the leader of the company can't get excited about the customer service initiative, how could he possibly expect employees to be excited about it?

Let's look at another positive example. A banking client was hosting a customer service initiative launch for their team. The event was at night, attendance was mandatory, and all hourly employees were to receive pay for the time. Pretty standard stuff. But here's what wasn't standard. Because they knew many of their employees had children, the bank offered free childcare at a facility near the meeting location. And even then, if parents didn't feel comfortable with that arrangement, the company was willing to reimburse them for any costs incurred from hiring their own caretakers. When the leadership team came to the stage to discuss the importance of wowing customers and going the extra mile, employees didn't have to imagine what that looked like: they'd just experienced it.

## DO UNTO OTHERS AS YOU WANT DONE UNTO YOU

To remain in the marketplace, it's important for every employee in the company to treat each other the way they're expected to treat customers. And to be the best in the business, it must be a company-wide practice. A book entitled *Delivering Knock Your Socks Off Service*, by Kristin Anderson and Ron Zemke, offers this tip for determining who your internal customers are: "In your organization, your customer is whoever benefits from the work you do — or conversely, whoever suffers when your work is done poorly or not at all."

Every organization depends on internal coordination and cooperation to succeed. An employee benefits when each member of the team pitches in and looks out for the greater good. And ultimately, customers profit from this all-for-one and one-for-all attitude.

Lesson 3 presented some strategies for wowing customers:

1. Wow through know-how

2. Take notice; take action

3. Add flair through care

Guess what? Those strategies are just as applicable to internal customers as they are to external customers. With every internal interaction, imagine if employees did what they said they would do (and did it well), were responsive to the needs of other employees, and demonstrated genuine care.

Let's explore this a little further:

1. **Wow through know-how.** When a colleague's question is answered incorrectly, a department's software application is installed sloppily, or a fellow employee simply doesn't know how to do his job, the entire system breaks down. But when employees take the time to answer questions thoroughly, to install software correctly, and to master job skills, then the organization benefits tremendously from their expertise.

2. **Take notice; take action.** Being responsive to other team members is one of the most appreciated and

important traits we can exhibit. After all, being responsive to external customers is pretty hard when you can't get any cooperation within the organization. One of the most popular and, I believe, most destructive joke posters I often see in offices says: "Lack of planning on your part does not constitute an emergency on my part." I don't care how well we plan, sometimes things just fall apart, and, yes, sometimes things get overlooked during the planning. But the attitude described on that poster isn't just arrogant: it's an attitude that builds walls within organizations. And we don't need any more walls. On the other hand, each of us has probably messed up or had a problem and been rescued by another team member. Whenever that happened to me, I know I was willing to do just about anything in return for that help.

3. **Add flair through care.** I remember a particular receptionist who worked in the Magic Kingdom Maintenance Department. Whenever I or anyone else called to report a problem, she not only got the information to the maintenance crew immediately, she was also a delight to talk to. Her tone of voice and overall demeanor made me feel good. Adding care to the equation puts heart into the operation. I can always tell when an organization's employees genuinely care for each other. There's a feeling of warmth, energy, and fun. Care can be demonstrated by something as simple as listening to

a fellow employee who needs to vent or as heroic as driving from Orlando to Tampa to return a colleague's misplaced and needed laptop computer.

One of the ways Disney World fostered a sense of internal care and service was through their cross-utilization program. Twice a year, during busy seasons in the parks, backstage cast members were assigned to work an onstage shift. It might have been a shift bussing tables, sweeping streets, scooping ice cream cones, or helping with crowd control. (For some of us they just tried to find a job where we couldn't hurt anyone). Not only did cross-u help deal with busy times, it also reconnected those who usually worked backstage to the real purpose of the organization — the guest experience. I know I was always reminded of how hard some of those onstage jobs were. After working a cross-u shift, I was certainly more empathetic to the challenges those cast members faced every day.

One of the ways world-class organizations become and stay that way is by creating great experiences for customers and by making their organization a great place to work. Turf wars, backstabbing, and finger-pointing aren't tolerated. Each employee is treated like a customer.

### Everyone Has a Customer

## QUESTIONS FOR APPLYING LESSON 8

1. How effective are your organization's employees at treating each other as customers? *MOSTLY*

2. When an internal service breakdown occurs in your organization, what is the impact on external customers? *LOSING BUSINESS, THEY DON'T WANT TO DEAL W/US AGAIN - TELLING OTHERS -*

3. Who are *your* internal customers?

4. What would excellent internal service look like in your role, department, or organization? *TO TREAT EVERYONE AS I EXPECT TO BE TREATED - OPEN COMMUNICTION, EFFECTIVE,*

5. What are some actions your organization should take in order to reinforce the importance of internal customer service? *TO BE ATTENTIVE TO THEIR SEROUNDING AND TAKE ACTION IF THEY SEE UNACCEPTABLE TREATMENT -*

* * * *

CONVERSATION
CONSULTATION
OPTIONS

# Figure Out What Ticks Off Your Customers — and Do Something About It

## SOMETIMES THE MAGIC JUST DOESN'T WORK

It was rare for me to see grown-up guests at Disney World without cameras – be it fancy video cameras, credit-card sized digital cameras, or disposable cameras (and now, of course, the ever-present smart phones). That's because Disney magic makes great memories. I've seen guests take photos (or taken the photos myself) of such moments as:

- A couple getting engaged in front of Cinderella's Castle

- A child getting his first haircut at the Main Street Barbershop

- An elderly couple waltzing down Main Street USA

- A young girl being chosen to be the "guest director" of the German Pavilion's band.

## SOME MEMORIES SHOULDN'T LAST A LIFETIME

But I also noticed some less-than-magical situations — the ones guests would just as soon forget when their Disney vacations were over — that crept into the mix. The cost, for example, can be quite shocking. Today a single day's admission is over $100. (When Disneyland opened in 1955, guests complained about the exorbitant entry fee: it was $1.00.) Beyond the entry fee, most guests buy food and drinks for their whole families, and $8 hotdogs, $3 fries, and $4 soft drinks add up quickly. Then there are the Disney souvenirs. Lots of them. That the exits of most of the major rides dump you right smack in the middle of a merchandise shop is no coincidence. After riding the Pirates of the Caribbean attraction, what young boy wouldn't beg to purchase a Captain Jack Sparrow costume? And what doting parent wouldn't consent? Consider the sweatshirt sales on a cold day and the poncho sales on a wet day. No one can accuse Disney of being a nonprofit organization.

But the cost of things is just one contributor to guests' not-so-magical memories. How about sweating in the steamy Florida sunshine, growing blisters on your feet from walking back and forth over a place so huge, or perhaps losing a wallet with all of your money in it or a pair of prescription glasses? How about promising your children a ride on Space Mountain only to discover it's closed for repairs? How about being stuck on a ride when it breaks down, having to listen to something like *It's a Small World* over and over again for thirty minutes or more until the problem is fixed. Yes, there's enchantment galore, but there are *in ABUNDANCE* also some potential frustrations that come with a vacation at Disney World. Like I said earlier, nothing is perfect, not even Disney magic! Out of all the frustrations, though, the number one most complained-about experience at Disney is — you guessed it — waiting in line.

Disney lines are legendary. When I worked there, guests often waited two hours or more to ride some attractions during peak times of the year. Life-long friendships developed as guests repeatedly passed each other winding through the queues.

For Disney, long lines meant good business and a lot of profit. But guests viewed it differently. Waiting in line was time that could be better spent doing other things, and when the lines weren't managed well, guests legitimately got ticked off. I met people who vowed never to return because of all the waiting.

This line issue is not unique to Disney. In fact, line management has become a focus of many hospitality, retail, and restaurant businesses in the last few years. Operational leaders attend seminars on this topic, and front-line workers continue to serve up ideas to improve wait time. Progressive hospital administrators are examining the issues of ER wait times and are looking at ways to reduce this added anxiety for patients and their families.

Over the years Disney took many steps to ease line frustration. Straightforward approaches included shading guests standing in line from the sun with canopies and simply keeping the lines moving. There is a psychological effect that makes people think as long as a line is moving, they are closing in on their goal. Signage let guests know how long the wait would be, managing expectations. Another Disney strategy was to fudge the information on the wait time signs. For example, a sign might show a thirty-minute wait for an attraction, while it was actually more like twenty-five minutes. When this happened, guests felt like they had beaten the system or received a gift.

In addition, Disney applied more sophisticated approaches to the line issue. At newer attractions, the line has been incorporated into the show. My favorite example is the Twilight Zone Tower of Terror at Disney's Hollywood Studios. This popular ride is themed around a fictional 1930's hotel that was struck by lightning, causing all of the guests to mysteriously disappear. When park guests wait to board the ride, they are treated to and become part of a fabulous exhibit. First, they're led into the hotel lobby where they see cobwebbed fixtures, half-full wine glasses, rotted food on tables, and other clues that underline the inherent drama. Next, guests enter a library where a video featuring Rod Serling of *Twilight Zone* fame tells the tragic story of what occurred the night the hotel was struck by lightning. They then progress through the basement boiler room complete with expected hissing sounds and sights. Guests love this, and many take pictures along the way. Of course, this fun hotel walk-through is really a wait in line. Disney cleverly made the line an innovative part of the show, and guests actually miss some of the intended experience if they don't wait at least a few minutes.

But the greatest and most sophisticated achievement in reducing line rage has been Fastpass™ — a process where guests can make reservations to go on major attractions, reducing wait times dramatically. A Fastpass can trim down a potential hour-long wait to only five minutes. Guests love it!

Fastpass resulted from the simple strategy of finding out what ticked off customers and doing something about it. That's an important lesson for every business. There's hardly an industry that doesn't have lines customers must wait in, whether in person or on the phone. Think about it. There are lines at the grocery store, at the Department of Transportation (renewed your driver's license lately?), and at Starbucks — especially in the morning. But if it isn't lines, every industry has some kind of frustrating aspect. What really infuriates customers, however, is when companies recognize what ticks customers off and then make absolutely no effort to remedy the problem. MAKING ANGRY

Entire industries regularly ignore customer frustrations and suffer greatly as a result. For example, you can be pretty sure if you have a 1 p.m. doctor appointment, you probably won't come close to seeing him or her before 1:45. Waiting rooms are crowded with fuming patients. Then, doctors have the audacity to charge patients a fee if they don't cancel an appointment at least twenty-four hours in advance. *Never* agree to that, by the way, unless the doctor is willing to reduce his fee for every minute he makes you wait beyond your appointment time. Fair is fair.

So, how does Disney find out what ticks off guests? Get ready; here it comes. They ask. Disney has multiple listening posts to find out what irritates guests. They survey guests as they leave the park about the pros and cons of their experience. Disney sends questionnaires to hotel guests following their stay. Each park has a Guest Relations Department to handle complaints. Disney Imagineers (what Disney calls their engineers) observe guests in the park to gain an understanding of what delights and frustrates them. And, of course, management regularly asks cast members to share their insights from working with the guests. When, for instance, Disney made the unfortunate decision to decorate Cinderella's Castle like a giant birthday cake in celebration of the park's twenty-fifth anniversary (Pepto Bismol pink for an entire year!), the cast was quick to let management know guests weren't too pleased. I don't think they'll do anything like that again.

The point here is to find out how your customers are feeling. Preferably before something causes angst or a mistake happens — like spending millions to paint a castle pink and install giant chocolate sprinkles on the turrets. It really was a horror.

Here are some other examples of what ticked off Disney guests and what the company did about it:

- The Florida heat can be unbearable during the summer. The moment you step outdoors sweat begins pouring from your body. In the Southwest they talk about dry heat. Well, in Florida the humidity makes for a very uncomfortable "wet heat." Disney incorporated plenty of shade in the parks with a lot of trees, awnings, and covered sitting areas. The queues were designed to get guests indoors, or at least under ceiling fans, as quickly as possible. In some locations they've installed mist machines so guests can get a blast of cool water as they walk the parks.

- Many children become frustrated when they can't find their favorite Disney character. So, the parks instituted a character hotline so any cast member can tell a guest exactly where to find Jasmine, Stitch, or Dopey. They also created designated character greeting locations where guests can find the perennial favorites like Mickey and Minnie.

- Some Disney attractions have height restrictions for safety reasons. Signs announce the restrictions before guests enter the queue and also throughout the line. But some guests are either oblivious to the warnings or choose to ignore them, thinking they'll sneak their under-the-limit child onto the ride. Being told by a cast member at the boarding area, potentially after queuing for an hour (an entertaining line or not), that the child won't be able to ride — well, it's meltdown time. Two solutions were introduced to manage the disappointment. First, some of the family members are asked to stay with the child while the rest of the family rides. When they return, those who had stayed behind hand over the child and take their turn with no additional wait. That certainly takes care of those who are tall enough to ride, but what about the child who isn't? Disney created colorful Future Rider certificates to give these under-height children, so on their next Disney vacation, when they've grown enough, they could present the certificate and go right to the front of the line! Many a potentially ruined vacation has been saved by these simple but powerful pieces of paper.

Now, none of these ideas were hatched by any great stroke of genius. As I have said, they came about because employees simply listened to what guests complained about and did something about it. Sitting back and saying, "Oh well, that's just the way it is, and customers will have to live with it," is the kiss of death. Listening and taking action are the keys to survival amongst the competition.

## WHAT ELSE TICKS PEOPLE OFF OUT THERE

Think about some of the companies you've done business with recently. I'll bet there were plenty of times you just shook your head wondering why they did things the way they did.

Here's an example. A neighbor was having some work done on his property and the workmen accidentally cut the buried phone lines leading to my house. We have a line for our private phone as well as several for our business. All were cut. On my cell phone, I called the phone company and went through the standard, and irritating, phone tree of "press one" for this and "press two" for that. Once I had made my selection, I waited on hold for twenty minutes, all the while hearing a recorded voice saying how important my call was. Right.

When a representative finally picked up, I explained the problem. He said they could have a technician out the next day to repair the residential line.

"But what about my business lines?" I asked.

"You'll have to talk to the small business department for that." And, of course, go through the same hassle of getting to a live person.

"Wait a minute," I said, "do the same technicians handle the residential and business line repairs?"

"Yes."

"Then why can't *you* just schedule the whole thing?"

The representative's reply: "Because that's not the way our system works."

Well, that's the way their system *should* work.

No wonder customer loyalty is so rare today, especially with phone companies.

OK, I've got one more phone company example to get off my chest. When I started my business and set up a phone line for it, the phone company neglected to tell me that the most recent owner of the line was a Papa Johns Pizza parlor. I spent the first year of my business handling a mix of calls asking for my consulting services and large pepperoni pizzas. You *know* they had to have had that information in their records and could have retired that number for awhile. Phone companies have to know what ticks off customers, so why don't they do something different? It all comes down to an organization understanding what drives customer loyalty and caring enough to do something about it. You can't have your blinders on to customer irritations.

All right, I actually have one more negative example from the phone company, this one I read in a newspaper. A customer disputed a $9 charge on his phone bill. The company wouldn't budge, so the customer canceled his service and switched to a competitor. The original company tried to lure the customer back, including a $50 credit as an incentive. Now, I'm no accountant, but this scenario doesn't make much financial sense to me.

Solving customer issues isn't always easy, but winning companies focus on eliminating their frustrations. Customers show their appreciation with their loyalty and their money. Consider these examples of understanding customer frustrations and taking action to fix the problem:

- A Cummins truck repair shop heard grumblings from truck drivers that they had to wander the lot to find their vehicles after a repair. The repair shop technicians recommended and took on the responsibility of pulling ready-for-pick-up trucks around to the front of the building and personally handing the keys to the drivers. It wowed the truck drivers and gave the technician an opportunity to discuss the repair and make sure the customer was satisfied with the work.

- Drive-through teller lines at banks can be pretty busy on Friday afternoons, resulting in high customer irritation. One solution, of course, would be to add more drive-through lanes — albeit an expensive solution. One bank tried an experiment. They hired high school students to come to the bank after school and serve fresh baked chocolate chip cookies to customers as they waited in their cars. Customers loved it, the students made a little cash, and the bank has made it a regular part of their Friday operation.

- A move to a new town or city can be stressful, especially if it entails your child starting a new school. Family friends recently went through such a move, with their son attending a new high school. The school, aware of and genuinely concerned about the impact of change on teenagers, had a program in place in which upper classmen acted as goodwill ambassadors. These ambassadors were carefully selected and trained to help new students feel comfortable with the school, get to know the lay of the land, and meet new friends.

- A common complaint in hospitals is the quality and availability of food. Forward thinking hospitals now offer twenty-four hour room service with an extensive menu from which patients and family members can order. Dietary restrictions are built into the system, and patient satisfaction regarding food typically skyrockets after this service is introduced.

- No matter where I am, I like to start my day at Starbucks. I like the people, the atmosphere, and the coffee. The line is usually long in the mornings, but I appreciate the efficiency with which employees keep it moving. They make eye contact with waiting customers, ask for orders about three to four people deep in the line, and acknowledge regulars. One time when I made it to the front of the line and ordered my grande decaf coffee (no fancy drinks for me), I was told the decaf was still brewing and would be ready in about five minutes. What could have been a mild irritation became a mild delight when the barista told me there is no charge if a customer has to wait for the coffee to brew. It turns out this is Starbucks' standard practice.

- You know the routine when you visit a doctor for the first time. You spend the first half hour filling out volumes of paperwork asking for your complete medical history (including specific dates of every illness as if you can remember) and your insurance information (five pages right there). Then there are the various disclaimers you must sign to guarantee there is no way you will ever, ever sue the doctor. A friend told me she had scheduled an appointment with a new doctor and was emailed all of the forms so she could complete them in advance. Why don't they all do that?

Each of these examples comes from organizations that understand solving customer frustrations is a great way to differentiate themselves from the competition. Most companies can't be bothered to figure out what ticks off their customers, much less make the commitment to address annoying issues.

## FINDING OUT AND FIXING IT

What are you, your company, or your department doing that just doesn't make sense or that annoys customers? Sometimes we've been doing something for so long we forget how frustrating it can be to customers. Other times we've decided that our convenience is more important than the customer's experience. How about the appliance repair company that says they'll be at your house sometime between 1 and 5 p.m.? Whose convenience are they concerned with? Most of us don't have time to sit around for four hours waiting for a repairman to show up. What if you told the repair company to have their technician sit in your driveway; you'll be home sometime between 1 and 5 p.m.? How agreeable do you think they'd be to that scenario?

Doing something to fix customer irritants isn't solely the responsibility of management. It should be everyone's responsibility to notice customer challenges and find ways to improve a process. For example, a gas station was receiving numerous complaints about overflowing trashcans and litter around the property. The problem was that there were over twenty receptacles on the property and lugging each one to the dumpster took an enormous amount of employees' time — often preventing them from completing other duties like serving customers. An employee came up with the idea of getting a cart that held twenty trashcan liners and they could then make one circuit of the property, change out every liner, and empty the full ones in a matter of minutes. The manager had been prepared to add staff or hire an outside service. The problem was solved by someone who knew it was his responsibility to do the job, but figured out a way to do it more efficiently.

One strategy I recommend to my clients is to hold employee focus groups at least once per quarter (preferably once per month) with nothing on the agenda except a discussion of customer frustrations and potential ways to alleviate them. Two things are accomplished this way: the customer experience is improved, and employees feel their input is valuable. Besides, employees know what's broken even more than customers do! They're the ones who see it each and every day.

The lesson in this chapter can be expanded from finding out what ticks off your customers and acting on that information to figuring out what ticks off your own employees and doing something about it. Remember, employees should be treated the way they're expected to treat customers. For example, when I was at Disney World, the park stayed open three hundred sixty-five days a year and was a twenty-four hour operation. Doing routine things, like buying stamps or cashing checks, could be a challenge for us as cast members. So, the company created opportunities for us to take care of these transactions on site. We could buy movie tickets, process film, register to vote, take classes, buy car insurance, and take care of a host of other errands without ever leaving the property. Many colleges have adopted this service-oriented campus approach, and they are finding it is a key differentiator when high school graduates (and their parents!) start weighing school options.

Most service innovations or process improvements happen because someone said, "Hey, you know what we should do? We should…" It may have been an executive or it may have been the person playing Mickey Mouse who came up with the idea — it doesn't matter. Everyone has a responsibility to make the place better for customers and for employees.

Consider what you already know that ticks off your customers (or your employees). Then think about how long it has been happening. Now, imagine how fixing those problems could positively impact the organization. While it's unrealistic to solve every problem, a few at a time can be taken on. Start with the ones that matter the most or the ones that exasperate the most. Customers and employees will appreciate the effort, and doing so will set you apart from the competition. Customers will think, "Why can't other companies do it like they do?"

### *Figure Out What Ticks Off Your Customers — and Do Something About It*

---

**QUESTIONS FOR APPLYING LESSON 9**

1. What are some frustrating processes you've endured as a customer? *IT CHANGE TASKS, NOT CONSIDERED THEIR FAULT—*

2. How do you react when you experience processes that are designed for a company's convenience rather than yours?

3. What do customers find frustrating about doing business with your organization? *NOT GETTING QUICK RESPONSE TO THEIR 1ST TIME TO # REQ.*

4. Are you asking customers about their experience with your organization? *NO*

   • If so, what are you learning?

   • What are you doing about it?

   • If you're not asking, when and how can you start?
   *I AM NOT SURE*

   (Continued on the next page)

---

5. What are your competitors (or even other
   industries) doing to make things easier for
   customers? What can you learn from them?
   I DON'T KNOW -
6. What can your organization do to encourage greater
   sharing of ideas for improving the customer
   experience? I AM NOT SURE,

*   *   *   *

## L E S S O N   1 0

# *Take Responsibility for Your Own Career*

### ASK AND YOU SHALL RECEIVE

Tony and I joined the Disney organization at the same time and met during new-hire orientation. A recent immigrant from England, where he had owned a pub, Tony wanted a career with Disney. While I was assigned to the 20,000 Leagues Under the Sea attraction, Tony went off to drive the antique cars on Main Street USA.

I saw Tony many times over the next several years. He was having the time of his life. While he had no desire to be in management, Tony did want his career at Disney to be stimulating, and to that end, he gave one hundred percent every day as a Disney host and driver. But, he also volunteered for every special

119

assignment that came along, and he soon had a reputation as the go-to person for any out-of-the-ordinary project. And most of those projects turned out to be pretty cool. Pretty soon, I rarely saw him driving those antique cars.

One time, I saw him escorting a film crew through the park, helping them get the shots they needed. Another time I saw Tony with a visiting celebrity, arranging photo sessions and interviews. Yet another time I bumped into him on the opening crew of a new attraction. Tony was having more fun than anyone I knew, and I wanted to know his secret. How was he getting all these great assignments? When I asked him, his answer was brilliant and a great lesson for anyone who wants to grow and love what they do. He said, "I asked."

I asked! Those two words, while simple, are keys that open the door of success. The secret, or principle here, is that you are responsible for your own career. No one is going to care more about your future than you. No one is going to tell you exactly what you need to do to be happy. In other words, no one can delegate his or her own success. Each of us needs to take the reins and make it happen. We have to ask.

Disney World employs over 60,000 cast members — a lot of people. So, you can well imagine that every time a special opportunity or an open position comes along, there's a lot of competition! Getting lost in such a vast sea of employees is easy, and many do — often due to their own negligence. Some employees wait to be discovered; they wait to be noticed; they wait to be given more responsibility. They wait, but they never ask.

You've probably seen this happen a few, if not countless, times in your own organization. Some employees believe things should just happen without doing what it takes to make them happen. And each time they get passed over for a promotion or assignment, they grow more bitter and begin a downward spiral into self-pity or doubt. And the more discouraged they become, the more doomed they are for any chance at the next opportunity.

Tony, on the other hand, asked. And the reason he got what he asked for was because people knew he could perform. After asking, the next step and key ingredient in taking responsibility for your own career is to act. Act like a professional; act like someone willing to learn; work hard; be a team player; go the extra mile. In essence, taking action is taking ownership. Tony's prior performance told bosses he was a dedicated, smart, hard worker. He took action. So, when he asked for a new assignment the answer was usually, "Absolutely," because people knew Tony would deliver. And he did deliver, time after time.

Too many people have the attitude, "Give me the job, then I'll show you what I can do." Life doesn't usually work that way, does it? We have to show what we can do before an organization is going to hand us that rewarding assignment. Sure, management should always be on the lookout for talent and provide opportu-nities for employees to learn and advance. But the ultimate responsibility lies with the employee. We have to take charge of our own careers.

Some say that the only path to making more money in an organization is the management path. But, career advancement isn't just about promotions into those positions. There are a lot of people who don't want to become managers; and there are a lot of other people who shouldn't. Advancement can take the form of new roles, new responsibilities, training opportunities, special projects, or anything else that enhances job satisfaction and pay — as with Tony.

Consider Roy, a cast member from my theme park days. Roy was a great employee, could always be counted on, and worked hard at whatever he did. He had no interest in moving into a management position, yet early in his career he had set high financial goals for himself. To reach those goals, he not only would've had to move into a management position, he pretty much would have had to run the place. To achieve his financial goal, Roy, instead, started buying run-down homes, fixing them up, and turning them into rental properties. All the while he was doing what he loved at Disney, and he never had to manage employees. With his side business going too, his net worth skyrocketed. Roy took responsibility for his own career.

Another colleague (and close friend) did choose a leadership career path. Patricia started at Disney World in 1983 as a waitress at Epcot and from there she moved up in the company, eventually managing a division of the Disney Vacation Club. She left Disney in 1997 and by 2003 was one of the top executives at Wyndham International. Patricia is brilliant and one of the most voracious learners I've ever met, but that alone didn't guarantee her success. The business world is full of smart people who are stalled in jobs they hate. Patricia took charge of her career and made things happen.

I asked her how she went from being a waitress to a Fortune 500 senior executive. Patricia said she saw every job as preparation for a future one — an opportunity to learn. Even if a job didn't pay as well as she would've liked, she gained knowledge and experience that helped her progress. In addition to building good relationships, Patricia got to work early, did more than was expected, and contributed good ideas. She volunteered for jobs no one wanted, and she did them well. She also worked on perfecting her writing, organizational, and presentation skills because she knew they would be helpful no matter the business or industry. These actions propelled Patricia from an entry-level position to the top of the corporate ladder in a relatively short time.

The career choices for Tony, Roy and Patricia were clearly different, but the code of success for them was similar. They all took responsibility for their own careers and didn't feel anyone owed them anything. They knew what they wanted and they went after it.

## I THINK I'LL WHINE INSTEAD...

And then there are the whiners. Employees who complain about everything, cause their bosses endless headaches, and then complain that they aren't appreciated. They decide that those who do move ahead or get the good assignments must be "brown noses," or "suck ups." They don't consider that just maybe those who do get ahead do so because they earned it.

Here are some of the more common complaints heard from employees who focus more on whining than contributing:

- *"It isn't fair. I've been here longer than she has."* A company should indeed value and reward employee loyalty. But when something needs doing, or someone's going to get promoted, smart managers turn to the employee who can and will do the job, and that isn't always the person who has stuck around the longest.

- *"Around here it's all about who you know."* Of course it is. Why would you expect it to be any different? How can someone select you for a job if he or she doesn't even know who you are? If it is all about who you know, then get to know people! Take ownership of building key relationships.

- *"Why does that department get to…(whatever it is they get to do)?"* This one drove a fellow manager of mine crazy. He just wouldn't tolerate that kind of whining. When someone gave him the "why do they get to…" complaint, he would always reply with, "If you want what they get, then do what they do." If you want what marketing reps get, then become a marketing rep. A lot of employees would be more successful if they stopped focusing on so-called injustices and focused more on their own performance.

- *"They just won't give me a chance."* They do give you a chance. Every day you have the same chance as everyone else in the company. Some people take advantage of the opportunity and show what they're capable of. But some blow the opportunity by failing to realize they were given a chance in the first place. They are simply too busy whining.

What I'm talking about here is a victim mentality. I'm sure you know people who go through life feeling victimized by their boss, the company, or the world. Everyone is out to get them, and they can't get a break. On the other hand, I'm sure you know someone who has faced challenging, even devastating circumstances, and in spite of this, has managed to stay focused, take responsibility, and forge ahead. So what's the difference? Those who succeed don't see themselves as victims. They see themselves as powerful and in charge of their lives and their careers. While they may certainly experience setbacks along the way, they don't see those obstacles as evidence of defeat or cruel intentions. Instead they see a setback as something to be reflected upon, dealt with, and overcome. Sure, they might have a few moments of self-pity, but they don't stay there. They get up, dust themselves off, and get back to work.

Companies and bosses love employees who take charge of their own careers. Responsible self-starters are a welcome relief from the whiners. Remember Tony? Here was a guy who could be counted on to do a great job and never waited around for things to happen! Roy didn't complain that he was not making enough money. Rather than whining about the Disney pay, or thinking he was entitled to more, he figured out a way to supplement his income. And Patricia made herself indispensable by focusing on the value she could add to each organization she worked for. These three were never victims.

The opposite of the victim mentality is the entitlement mentality. A lot of people think they're entitled to things they are actually not entitled to. They think they're entitled to a raise, a bonus, a promotion, a company car, a private jet — the list goes on and on. They are the employees who drain everyone's energy because they see everything as a problem or injustice and feel the need to express this to everyone around them. Guess what? We're entitled to a good day's pay for a good day's work. We make a deal with the company when we sign up, and anything above and beyond that deal is a reward for our having gone above and beyond.

The victim and entitlement mentalities are career killers. People infected with these outlooks do have something in common — they don't see that they have to earn success in both effort and attitude. Most companies and bosses waste far too much time dealing with victims and demanders.

So, thank goodness for the go-getters — those employees who are inspiring to be around, do what needs to be done (without complaining or demanding), and somehow make everyone's life easier. Bosses will do just about anything for them.

## TAKING CHARGE

Here are a few tips for taking charge of your career:

- **Let your boss know your goals.** Don't assume your boss knows what you want. If you're interested in a promotion, additional responsibilities, or a new opportunity, tell your leader. Just taking the initiative to let your boss know what you want to do sets you apart from ninety percent of employees who sit back waiting for something good to happen.

- **Be a problem solver.** Bosses love employees who eagerly tackle challenges. There is a long line out the boss's door of employees who complain about problems. The line of employees with solutions is much shorter and much more welcome. By the way, bringing problems to light is OK. But there is a huge difference between alerting your boss to a problem and whining about one. If there's a real problem, you can be certain a leader wants to know about it, but they also want some help in fixing it. I read some advice somewhere that said, "Become known for the problems you solve." What great advice! When you become the go-to person who can help solve business challenges, people are going to do more to help your career. Become known for the problems you solve.

- **Find a mentor.** Having a mentor is about learning from someone who is, or has been, where you want to be. I've had many mentors, and some of them didn't even know they played that role. In fact, some of them were dead. For instance, I've learned a lot about

creativity, persistence, and passion for quality from
Walt Disney, and he died before I was seven years old.
Other mentors were bosses; others were co-workers.
None were perfect but I learned something from each
of them. Most were very generous with their time and
flattered to be asked for help and guidance. It goes
back to our lesson at hand — asking. Most people simply don't.

- **Be passionate about your work.** Employees with
  real passion stand out from those who simply put in
  time. You know them the minute you watch them
  work because they clearly care. You can see it in their
  eyes, hear it in their words, and observe it in their
  actions. I'm not talking about over-the-top, bounce-
  off-the-walls type of passion. Passion like that is usually irritating to co-workers and customers. I'm
  talking about sincere passion that shines through in
  great work and genuine care.

- **Always learn.** People who feel they know it all and
  have seen it all are in big trouble. The world of business is changing too fast for you to ever rest on your
  laurels. I was once fired from a job (actually I quit
  because I heard I was about to be fired) because I
  stopped learning. As a teenager I worked in a hardware store and figured I knew how to stock shelves
  and run the cash register. But I didn't learn everything
  I should've about the products we sold and quickly
  outlived my usefulness. It was certainly a humbling
  experience, and I vowed it would never happen again.
  Opportunities for learning are everywhere. Every
  trade or profession has its magazines; physical
  and virtual bookstores are filled with books about

every element of business; training classes and seminars are offered every day. There's no good excuse for not learning.

A seatmate on a flight once took advantage of the three-hour flying time by complaining to me about his company and how he was stuck in his career. The company didn't care about him, didn't send him to training, didn't, didn't, didn't. I subtly suggested that he get some training on his own or read some books on his trade. He said, "I'll go to the classes and read the books if the company pays me for the time." No wonder his career had stalled. His attitude was that he would only learn if the company paid him to. Well you do get paid for learning, it's just that the money comes later. Learning is a sure investment.

- **Make your boss look good.** A lot of people hate to hear this one, thinking, "My boss is a pain in the butt. Why should I make him look good?" Because if you make the boss look bad, chances are you'll look bad, too. And bad-mouthing the boss puts you down in the mud with the whiners. Setting your boss up for success isn't sucking up — it's smart.

- **Work hard and smart.** A popular saying goes, "Don't work harder, work smarter." I actually hate that phrase because people think it means anything goes as long as the work gets done. One business author claimed that as long as her employees got their work done, she didn't care if they played video games or golf all afternoon. That's just talk. I've yet to meet a CEO or manager who doesn't value employees who work hard and don't goof off. I'm all for working smarter because it opens up time to get more things done. But being known as a person who gets to work early and burns the midnight oil when necessary sets you apart from those who punch a clock — literally and figuratively.

- Show up on time or early. I love the old Woody Allen quote, "Ninety percent of success is just showing up." I don't know if the percentage is right, but the sentiment sure is. When I was a supervisor in the character department I'd spend the morning handling calls from entertainers who weren't coming in to work because of illness. Usually the absences were legitimate, but there were some cast members who simply didn't want to come to work. And it was the same offenders over and over. It was almost comical to hear the rehearsed routines about how sick they were and listen to the forced hacking, phony sneezing, and all of the other fabricated symptoms.

There's an old saying that there are three kinds of people: those who make things happen, those who watch things happen, and those who wonder what happened. People who make things happen will always be in demand. They are not at the mercy of a single boss or a single company. They don't have to worry about a down economy or the effects of offshoring. They call the shots.

### *Take Responsibility for Your Own Career*

## QUESTIONS FOR APPLYING LESSON 10

1. What opportunities have you asked for lately? *To work on different project-*

2. What specifically have you done recently to gain new knowledge or skills in order to increase your value to your organization? *Consult on the issues that I have not dealt with before & gain knowledge about it*

3. What can you do to take more responsibility for your career? *I am not looking for a career!*

4. What can you do to ensure that your boss clearly understands your goals? *To let him know what I am interested to do. Communication*

5. Who are your mentors, and do they know your goals? *Aria and he knows my goals.*

6. If you have direct reports, what can you do to encourage them to take accountability for their own careers? *I do not have direct reports.*

7. Are you someone who makes things happen, watches things happen, or wonders what happened?

   * * * * *Make things happen —*

# *Conclusion*

Writing this book has been a wonderful, rejuvenating experience. Looking back at my time at Walt Disney World has reinforced the realization that I was truly fortunate to have worked there for twenty years. As I wrote in the introduction to this book, the lessons I learned at Disney have proved invaluable in my work and personal life, and I use each of these lessons just about every day. I owe a lot to Disney.

This is clearly not a huge book — it's a pretty quick read. A friend was kidding me asking, "Is this really all you learned in twenty years? Just these ten things?" Yes. These ten lessons comprise everything I learned at Disney. Or I should say, the core of everything I learned. Anything else is just an offshoot of these principles. My friend then asked, "Didn't you learn anything about hiring?" Yes, I learned to hire people who are likely to live these lessons. "What about training?" Yes, I learned it's important to teach employees how these lessons apply to their jobs. Communication, measurement, accountability, ownership —

every single one of the leadership skills I have developed (or have tried to develop) revolves around these ten lessons.

Think about any organization you deal with as a customer. Imagine if every employee lived all of these lessons every day. Wouldn't you become a loyal fan? Well, there are some organizations that do live these principles, and they're the ones recognized as world class. They're also the ones you love to do business with, as you pass by endless competitors who might be a bit more convenient but not nearly as valued.

I sincerely hope reading this book has been helpful to you as you think about your organization, your career, and your life.

I wish you the very best as you apply *Lessons From the Mouse.*

\* \* \* \*

# Acknowledgements

To my wife, Debbie, I want to thank you for your unwavering support during the writing of *Lessons From the Mouse*. I think you read the manuscript more times than I did and your patience was saint-like during the entire process. And to my two sons, Danny and David, I thank you both for being ongoing sources of inspiration, pride, and love.

To my parents, Dick and Marie Snow, you have supported my efforts throughout my life — even when I wanted to be a professional magician. You've always been there for me and are the embodiment of "unconditional love." You took me on my first visit to Walt Disney World and encouraged me to work there when my plan was to hitchhike to Colorado and live off the land in the mountains. Your idea was better.

Jonathan Pennell, your cover design and book layout certainly exceeded my expectations. Working with you has been a great partnership.

Caroline Bartholomew, thank you for bringing your expert editing skills to the process. Your creative input and attention to detail are certainly appreciated.

Finally, I'd like to thank all of the Walt Disney World cast members I had the privilege to work with during my twenty years "working for the mouse." The memories will always be treasured.

# *About The Author*

Dennis Snow spent twenty-years "working for the mouse" at Walt Disney World. Starting his Disney career at the 20,000 Leagues Under the Sea Attraction, he moved into a management position, managing various operating areas throughout the famous theme park. He also spent several years with the Disney University, teaching corporate philosophy and business practices to cast members and the leadership team.

Now a full-time speaker, trainer, and consultant, Dennis is dedicated to helping organizations achieve their goals in the areas of customer service, employee engagement, and leadership. Dennis can be contacted at *dennis@snowassociates.com*.and at *www.snowassociates.com*. You can read his commentaries at *www.dennissnowblog.com*.